Frontispiece

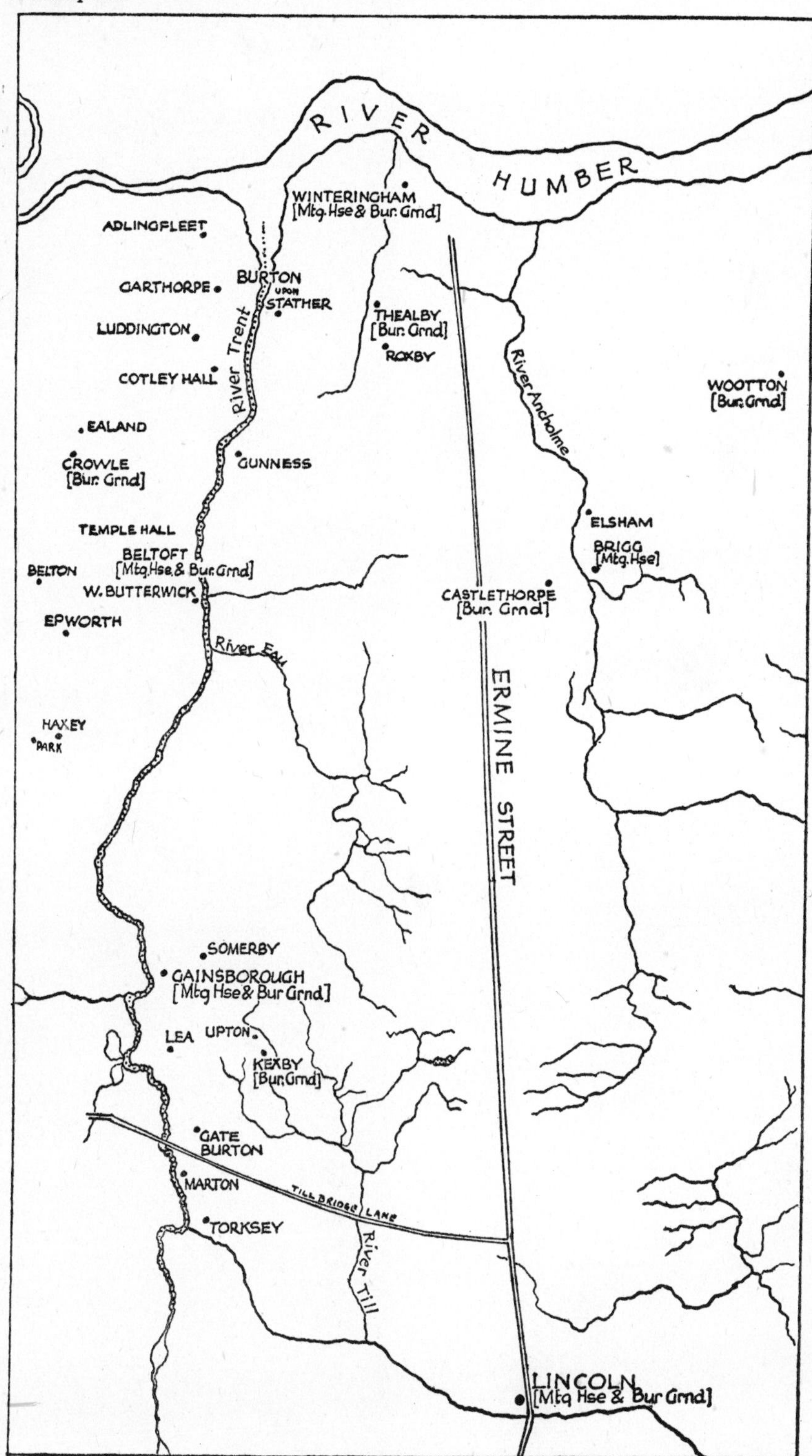

MAP OF PLACES MENTIONED IN THE TEXT

THE

PUBLICATIONS

OF THE

Lincoln Record Society

FOUNDED IN THE YEAR

1910

VOLUME 38

FOR THE YEAR ENDING 30TH SEPTEMBER, 1941

The First Minute Book of the Gainsborough Monthly Meeting of the Society of Friends

1669—1719

EDITED BY

HAROLD W. BRACE

Clerk of Lincolnshire Monthly Meeting

Volume I

1669–1689

PRINTED FOR

THE LINCOLN RECORD SOCIETY

BY

THE HEREFORD TIMES LIMITED, HEREFORD

1948

a1

TABLE OF CONTENTS

Gainsborough Preparative Meeting held 4th of eleventh month 1945.

Minute 7. This meeting raises no objection against the request of the Lincoln Record Society to publish the first Minute Book (1669–1719) of the former Gainsborough Monthly Meeting, and leaves Harold W. Brace at liberty to raise the matter at next Monthly Meeting.

Frank Marshall,
Clerk.

At a Monthly Meeting held at Lincoln on 7th day, the 10th of Eleventh Month 1945, at 2 p.m.

Minute 20. The Clerk brought before Monthly Meeting his concern to edit, for publication by the Lincoln Record Society, the earliest Minute Book (1669–1719) of the former Gainsborough Monthly Meeting. Monthly Meeting has unity with the Clerk in his concern and liberates him for that service.

Harold W. Brace,
Clerk.

INTRODUCTION

THE MANUSCRIPT

The Minute Book consists of 234 leaves of paper measuring $11\frac{1}{8}$ inches by $7\frac{3}{4}$ inches written on both sides, loosely enclosed within a leather cover, which, however, is not the original, for it is too small and has allowed the ends and one edge to project, thus causing a certain amount of damage by friction. Except for this damage, the condition of the book is good, and the writing in general is legible.

The Early History of the Gainsborough Monthly Meeting of the Society of Friends

It is commonly considered that Quakerism was founded by George Fox (born July 1624 at Fenny Drayton, Leicestershire—died in London 13th January, 1691), but this is an over-simplified statement. Rufus M. Jones has shown that what Fox, and his coadjutors, did was to crystallise into definite form, and give expression to, certain trends of thought which had been developing during the sixteenth and seventeenth centuries and to which many religious reformers had contributed.[1] Consequently, when Quakerism was introduced into an area which was, or had been, previously influenced by Non-Conformity, conditions conducive to favourable reception existed already.

George Fox was not a widely read man and probably absorbed most of his ideas unconsciously by intercourse with other religious exponents, especially during his period of intense spiritual travail. His connexions with the Baptists perhaps began with his uncle —Pickering—but it was in Nottinghamshire that he encountered a number of former adherents to that sect, who had split up into small groups (hence his term—Shattered Baptists) and he was, for a time, in spiritual fellowship with them, and they developed into the earliest Quaker congregation.

It is, therefore, of importance to consider where, and when, such predisposing influences existed when Quakerism was first preached in that part of Lincolnshire to which the volume of Minutes, now printed, relates. Among those who were suspended for not subscribing to the three articles in 1583–4 were: Thomas Bradley, Curate of Torksey, and his neighbour John Huddlestone,

[1] *Studies in Mystical Religion*, Rufus M. Jones, London, 1936. *Spiritual Reformers in the 16th and 17th Centuries*, Rufus M. Jones, London, 1914.

Vicar of Saxilby,[1] and John Julian, Vicar of Elsham, was presented for not wearing the surplice in 1585.[2]

Non-Conforming clergy in 1604 include William Harrison, Vicar of Marton,[3] and, doubtfully, Thomas Forman, Rector of Winteringham.[4] At Gainsborough (1607) "The minister is in all things conformable, savinge they never saw him weare a cornered cap or ride in a cloke with sleeves "[5] but we know that John Smyth the Se-Baptist, was then in the town, at the head of a Separatist Congregation. The following entries in the Parish Register appear to relate to him :—

"Mar. 11. 1603–4 Baptized Chara daughter of Mr. John Smith, preacher.

Mar. 7. 1605–6 Baptized Sarah daughter of John Smyth, Clerke."

We get a hint of the social standing of the early Separatists from Richard Bernard, Vicar of Worksop, who wrote that Smyth was pastor of "tradesmen in Gainsborough ".[6] Evidently his appeal was neither to the labouring poor nor to the gentry, but to the middle class of that day. Harassed by the ecclesiastical authorities, Smyth and his flock emigrated to Amsterdam in 1608, but this certainly did not empty the town of Dissenters for the Parish Register records the Burial on June 18, 1614, of : "Mercy, daughter of one Henry Cullen (or Coling) a Brownist " and on September 20, 1624, of "Roberte Shorte, a Brownist boreali ".

In, or before, the year 1629, the Master of the Gainsborough Grammar School, was one Hanserd Knollys who records :—
"a Providential acquaintance, that I had gotten with a very godly old widdow in Gainsburgh, where I taught the Free-School, who told me of one called a Brownist, who used to pray and expound Scriptures in his family, whom I went sometimes to hear, and with whom I had Conference, and very good Counsel ".[7] We have no means of knowing whether Hanserd Knollys' acquaintance was the Henry Cullen mentioned above, or perhaps Roberte Ebbatson, Brownist, whose burial is recorded in the Parish Register under the date February 23rd, 1630.

At all events, Henry Cullen lived on until the days of the Commonwealth, when Independency had become a power in the land, and he thus provided a living link with the days of the early Separatists. The record of his burial, in the Parish Register, reads "August 11th, 1655, Henry Cullin of Morton, a Sectary ".

[1] *The State of the Church in the Reigns of Elizabeth and James I*, ed. C. W. Foster, L.R.S. XXIII, Intro. pp. xxiv—xxv.
[2] *Ibid.*, p. xxx. [3] *Ibid.*, p. cviii. [4] *Ibid.*, p. cvii.
[5] *Ibid.*, p. lxxx. [6] *Vide infra.*
[7] *The Life and Death of that old disciple of Jesus Christ and eminent Minister of the Gospel, Mr. Hanserd Knollys*, pp. 4–5, London, 1692.

It has been possible to show this continuity of Dissenting influence in Gainsborough merely because the parochial records have been available for close detailed examination and, if similar intensive studies were made for the parishes of the Isle of Axholme, it may well be that other evidence of a like character would be forthcoming there also. In the absence of such studies, it has been suggested that " It is quite possible that the existing dissenting churches of Crowle, Epworth and Butterwick, in the Isle of Axholme, are derived from the labours of Smyth around Gainsborough ; though it is to be regretted that someone who saw this possibility proceeded to forge documents to support his theory. The genuine church-book of Epworth has lost its early pages, and only begins with 1676 ; but the followers of Smyth in Lincoln included Thomas Pigott from Axholme, who succeeded him as leader at the Bake-house ; we may be sure that he had friends left behind in the Isle ; and we may well think that some of them became bold enough to start a Baptist Church there. The solid facts are that such a community existed in 1626, that its letters of 1630 are at Amsterdam, that in 1634 the vicar-general of Laud certified to him that the members were numerous, and were led by Johnson, a baker ".[1]

Richard Bernard, Curate of Epworth 1597–8,[2] very nearly reached the Separatist position,[3] but drew back under episcopal disciplinary pressure and became involved in a controversy with John Smyth, for whom he coined the nickname " Se-Baptist "[4] and alleged that Smyth " was made Minister by Tradesmen ".[5]

The link suggested between early Non-Conformity in Gainsborough and the Isle of Axholme may have been determined by the natural line of communication—the Trent—and, in the same way, the Great North Road may have led to the existence of a group of Dissenters just south of Doncaster in succession to the Separatist congregation which met at Scrooby when Smyth was in Gainsborough.

This group of " Seekers ", at Balby, Warmsworth and Tickhill, had evidently moved far from the Baptist position, some indeed probably having achieved the Quaker experience before George Fox visited them and established the first really strong centre of Quakerism from which came such stalwarts as John and Thomas Killam, Thomas Aldam and Richard Farnsworth, who was second only to Fox himself in the Quaker leadership in the north. There is therefore some evidence of Dissenting influence before the actual introduction of Quakerism at Elsham, Gainsborough, Torksey, Marton, Crowle, Epworth, Butterwick and, perhaps, Winteringham.

1 *A History of British Baptists*, W. T. Whitley, London, 1923, p. 48.
2 L.R.S. XXIII, pp. 185, 330.
3 *Plaine Evidences*, Richard Bernard, 1610, p. 4.
4 *Ibid.*, p. 17. 5 *Ibid.*, p. 20.

As regards Dissent contemporary with the introduction of Quakerism, Non-Conforming Clergy who were ejected from their livings in 1660 included James Abdy,[1] Vicar of Elsham, and John Ryther,[2] Vicar of Frodingham (son of 'a pretty noted Quaker'). Amongst others who were deprived at "Black Bartholomew" in 1662 were:—

Robert Durant,[3] Rector of Risby cum Roxby and Vicar of Crowle,
Jonathan Grant,[4] Rector of Flixborough,
Mark Tricket,[5] Rector of Gate Burton, previously Vicar of Adlingfleet, Yorks.,
Thomas Bonner,[6] Rector of Lea,
— Aires,[7] Vicar of Glentworth,
Thomas White,[8] Vicar of Scawby.

There is also the interesting case of William Quipp, who had officiated at Marton and Torksey, and who became Non-Conformist after 1685.[9] The additional places are thus Frodingham, Roxby-cum-Risby, Flixborough, Adlingfleet, Lea, Glentworth, Scawby, at all of which there were Quakers in the earliest days of the movement.

George Fox was apprenticed to a shoemaker who was also a grazier; when 19 years old he became deeply conscious of a special mission from God and about 1646 gave up attendance upon Church Ordinances, contenting himself with the teaching of the Spirit. Two years later he began, at Manchester, to preach, urging men to cast aside as worthless, or even pernicious, all forms and ceremonies of worship, and to trust in the "Inner Light". This concept of the indwelling presence of God in the Soul, or "that of God in every man" as it is now expressed, is the basic tenet of Quakerism and, as misrepresented, seems to have provoked something like a riot at its first introduction to Gainsborough.[10] The subsequent calumny to which Fox refers was:—"One Cotten Crosland of Ackworth (neer Pontefract in Yorkshire) a professed Quaker, pretending that he knew far more, and higher things than ever any Minister did, or could discover to him, hang'd himself, and lies buried in a Crosseway upon Ackworth Moor, with a stake driven threw him, which may be as a standing mark to warn Passengers to take heed of quaking, seeing that Spirit, which is the cause of it, leads men into such fearful miscarriages".[11] Fox uses the word "professor" to mean an extreme and bigoted Puritan, the deriva-

[1] A. G. Matthews, *Calamy Revised*, Oxford, 1934, p. 1.
[2] *Ibid.*, p. 421. [3] *Ibid.*, p. 173. [4] *Ibid.*, p. 231.
[5] *Ibid.*, p. 493. [6] *Ibid.*, p. 64. [7] *Ibid.*, p. 4.
[8] *Ibid.*, p. 525. [9] *Ibid.*, p. 402.
[10] See Appendix in Vol. III under year 1652.
[11] *The Quakers Shaken, or a Warning against Quaking*, London, 1655.

tion is obscure but perhaps the sense is that of Titus 1, 16—" They profess that they know God; but in works they deny him, being abominable and disobedient, and unto every good work reprobate ".

Others soon followed up the initial visit of George Fox. John Whitehead held a Meeting at Butterwick in the first or second month of 1653,[1] then Richard Farnsworth and Thomas Killam together;[2] these two, from the group of " Seekers " in South Yorkshire, evidently drew a clear distinction between their " ould frends ", presumably other Seekers with whom they were in touch, and " Baptized ones " who had not abandoned Baptist principles.

In that same year there are the first three recognisable Quaker references in the Gainsborough Parish Register, the first of which, recording the birth of a child whose parents evidently refused baptism, illustrates the Quaker laying aside of Sacraments as being inconsistent with the working of the " Inner Light " of Christ in the heart without its having to be specially mediated for Salvation. Five similar references occur in the next year,[3] and then we have a sign of the times in the account of a debate at the residence of Justice Wray, at which Richard Farnsworth and James Naylor spoke for Quakerism. This has been ascribed to Glentworth,[4] but Wharton Hall (in Blyton Parish) seems more likely. Richard Farnsworth was in the neighbourhood again in 1656.[5] for there is a letter of his dated 20 : ix : 1656 from " Martine in Lincolnshire " (Marton) in which he is evidently adjudicating amongst Friends at Glentworth and Ingham, which exemplifies the high standard of conduct Quakers set for themselves.

To a Quaker, a line of conduct, which shows evidence of stricter interpretation of Christ's teaching than is observed by other denominations, is known as bearing Testimony; and Friends' Testimony against taking Oaths, based primarily on Matthew v, 34, also shows their dislike of a double standard of truthfulness, one for ordinary use and a higher one, after taking an oath, for legal purposes. The earliest illustration quoted is from 1655 but, later, this was to prove one of the costliest of Quaker Testimonies. The Toleration Act gave relief from the Oath of Allegiance and, in 1695, a form of affirmation was legalised for seven years, renewed in 1702 and made perpetual in 1715 (Geo. I, Cap. 6). The wording, however, was not satisfactory to all Quakers[6] and so caused much internal controversy, but a form of words which found general acceptance was conceded in 1722 (8 Geo. I, Cap. 6). The Restoration Year was, apparently, one of severe persecution under the head of oath-taking,[7] presumably the Oath of Abjuration would be the

[1] *The Written Gospel—Labours of that Ancient and Faithful Servant of Jesus Christ—John Whitehead*, London, 1704.
[2] See Appendix under year 1653.
[3] See Appendix under year 1654.
[4] William C. Braithwaite, *The Beginnings of Quakerism*, London, 1923, p. 198.
[5] See Appendix under year 1656.
[6] See text under date 6 : i : 1713.
[7] See Appendix under year 1660.

chief instrument, though the case from Adlingfleet shows that any oath would serve the purpose.

Only names from the Gainsborough Monthly Meeting have been quoted, and it will be seen that the Isle, with about 5 per cent. of the population of Lincolnshire (1676 census), had 30 per cent. of the prisoners, and Gainsborough and district, with 2 per cent. of the population, had 6 per cent.; as a rough approximation, therefore, at this time, Quakerism had made six times as much progress in the Isle of Axholme and three times as much in Gainsborough and district, as it had over the county as a whole.

A much sharper instrument of persecution was added by the second Conventicle Act of 1670 (22 Car. 11, cap. 1) which created two additional penalties, a fine of £20 for preaching at and a similar sum for harbouring a conventicle, and introduced the obnoxious principle of encouraging the informer who was to receive his share of the fines. The account of Gainsborough Friends' suffering under this Act contains two of those curious records of what was termed "Examples upon Persecutors", that is, what they considered the judgment of God upon those who troubled them. (Edward Laughton and Thomas Parnell.)

Since they believed that salvation could only come from "The true Light, which lighteth every man that cometh into the world" (John i, 9) it followed that they could only recognise a Ministry derived from this source and so a paid priesthood, which contravened Christ's command to those he sent forth to preach: "Freely ye have received, freely give" (Matthew x, 8) was particularly obnoxious to them. Therefore, since tithes were the usual means of support of the paid priesthood, they could not, in conscience, pay such demands and we have the earliest local instances of this Testimony from Crowle and Amcotts,[1] and in the same year an illustration of popular resentment against Quaker criticism of the diversions of the times—presumably cock-fighting, bull-baiting and the like. Fox deprecated "Wakes or feasts, May-games, sports, plays and shows",[2] "bowling, drinking, hunting, hawking"[3] and "shovel-board".[4]

With the restoration of the monarchy came the re-establishment of the power of the Episcopate and the beginnings of ecclesiastical as well as secular persecution. The first visitation of which we have a record after the Restoration contains names of Quakers from most of the parishes in the area, presented mainly for non-attendance at Church but also for such varied offences as not coming to be churched after child-birth, refusal of baptism, working on Saints' Days, not burying according to the rites of the established Church nor in the Church-yard, sitting in Church with the hat on, not

[1] See Appendix under year 1658.
[2] George Fox, *Journal*, Bi-Centenary Edition, London, 1902, Vol. I, p. 39.
[3] *Ibid.*, p. 325.
[4] *Ibid.*, Vol. II, p. 281.

marrying according to the practice of the Church of England, or quite simply for being Quakers. Most of these depend upon their objection to the external observances in worship and the intervention of a paid official in what they held should be a purely spiritual concern, but the refusal to remove the hat in deference to temporal authority, like most of the Quaker testimonies, had been practiced by others[1] before the introduction of Quakerism.

Since they refused the offices of the Church, Quaker births, burials and marriages would not normally appear in Parish Registers and they were obliged to create a registration system of their own. Some of the earliest entries in Friends' Registers have evidently been made retrospectively and to overlap the duplicate entries which are in the Parish Registers.

In the case of marriage something more than a mere system of registration was necessary and Quaker marriage procedure still shows strong resemblance to the civil form of declaration established by law in 1653 and abolished at the Restoration, and the legality of Quaker marriage was generally regarded as having been settled by a *nisi prius* action at Nottingham in 1661.[2] This precedent stood until 1844 when it was reversed by a decision in the House of Lords and thus necessitated the Act of 10 and 11 Vic., c. 58, validating these marriages *ex post facto*. The man under the Commonwealth procedure made the following declaration :—

> "I (A.B.) do here in the presence of God, the searcher of all hearts, take thee (C.D.) for my wedded wife, and do also, in the presence of God and before these witnesses, promise to be unto thee a loving and faithful husband,"

which may be compared with the Quaker declaration :—

> "Friends, in the presence of the Lord, I take this my Friend (C.D.) to be my wife, promising, through divine assistance, and so long as we both on earth shall live, to be unto her a loving and faithful husband,"

and it is important to observe that both men and women made precisely the same declaration. This is, of course, implicit in Quakerism, for "Inner Light" was obviously not a purely male prerogative and Quaker women enjoyed equality of status in all spiritual matters with their menfolk at a time when the position of women generally, both in law and in fact, was very inferior to that of men.

The declarations of marriage intentions which occur throughout the Minutes bear an obvious resemblance to the publication of banns, except that the procedure is positive in that enquiries as

[1] *Calendars of State Papers Domestic* (see Appendix under Year 1639).
[2] George Fox, *op. cit.*, Vol. I, p. 520.

to the absence of impediments to marriage were definitely made, whereas banns are negative in the sense that they stand good unless challenged. On one exceptional occasion, a young man was allowed to make a marriage declaration by proxy[1] but Monthly Meeting always inquired strictly into any seeming irregularity such as delay[2] or a broken engagement[3] and insisted, on the remarriage of a widow, that the rights of children, by her former husband, should be safeguarded.[4]

From 1662 we begin to get references to the persecution under what has been called " The Quaker Act " (13 and 14 Car. II, cap. 1) which imposed penalties for maintaining the unlawfulness of oaths and for meeting to the number of five or more : and the power of the Bishops being restored, we also find imprisonment following an issue of the writ *de Excommunicato Capiendo*. There was a certain lull in the intensity of persecution at the time of the Dutch war, the Great Plague and the Fire of London, although these events being somewhat remote, might not affect this area directly. In the same year (1667) that the Dutch fleet sailed into the Medway and in which Clarendon fell, George Fox, released from a long imprisonment in Scarborough Castle, went about the country setting up the Quaker organisation very much as it still exists to-day. The basis of Quaker organisation was the group of Friends who, meeting together regularly weekly for Worship, in a particular locality, comprised what was therefore termed a " Weekly " or " Particular " Meeting. Several such " Particular " Meetings were grouped together to form an administrative unit, each Particular Meeting sending one or more of its members as representatives to the administrative Meeting held Monthly and hence styled a " Monthly Meeting ", the area over which it had jurisdiction being " the Compass of the Monthly Meeting ". Two or more Monthly Meetings nominated representatives to regional Meetings, four times in the year, and so known as " Quarterly Meetings " and the limits of the Quarterly Meetings, as originally defined, followed, in general, the county boundaries. Finally, each Quarterly Meeting appointed annually its Representatives to a general Meeting for the whole country, held usually in London and thus called London Yearly Meeting, which was, and is, the supervisory body for the whole Society in this country. Fox constituted Lincolnshire a Quarterly Meeting and divided it into four Monthly Meetings which it is interesting to note, followed, mainly, existing civil or ecclesiastical boundaries, Lincoln Monthly Meeting corresponding roughly to Kesteven, Spalding Monthly Meeting to Holland and Gainsborough Monthly Meeting to the then Archdeaconry of Stow, the remaining portion of Lindsey comprising Mumby Monthly Meeting. A noteworthy omission from the

[1] See text under date 13 : v : 1683.
[2] See text under date – : ii : 1670.
[3] See text under date 10 : x : 1673.
[4] See text under date 12 : ii : 1689.

original setting out is that there is no mention of Brigg, which soon after became one of the strongest centres of Quakerism in Gainsborough Monthly Meeting.[1]

Perhaps the exact place of the meeting, as between Elsham and Brigg, was not settled. Brigg meeting was mainly composed of families whose names appear in the Elsham Register during John Julian's incumbency.

When gathered for business or disciplinary purposes, Quakers have, from the beginning of their organisation, kept records: and every such Meeting has an appointed Clerk, who combines the duties of Chairman and Secretary. A Clerk's function is to introduce the business, furnish the Meeting with relevant information necessary for adequate consideration, await the subsequent discussion, frame an appropriate minute embodying the general consensus of opinion (i.e., "take the sense of the Meeting") and, finally, read out his minute for approval or amendment. No vote is ever taken and, in harmony with that principle, a Clerk must beware of being influenced by mere numerical strength of expressed opinions on any debatable point, since the counsel of a single sagacious member of long experience ("a weighty Friend") may be of greater value than several counter opinions emanating from those of lesser capacity.

Keeping his mind thus receptive to the trend of the discussion, a Clerk cannot express his personal opinions but must confine himself to contributing factual matter and be ready to sink his individuality in the service of the Meeting. So that, although we can draw up the following list of Clerks who compiled this Minute Book: Robert Rockhill, to 1685; John Parsons and Thomas Markham, to 1686 (perhaps interim appointments); Joseph Richardson to 1716 and lastly John Oxley; we must not suppose that the minutes reflect the personalities of the successive Clerks, except in such details as handwriting, mode of expression, etc. In this connection, during the period 1679–1685, when Robert Rockhill actually signs the minutes, the penmanship is of remarkable quality; his spelling is good and his writing is in the Italian hand, an occasional long "s" being almost the only deviation from modern practice, and the writing is "copper-plate". For convenience, Clerks of Meetings make their original minutes in rough, at the actual Meeting, and a fair copy later; for this reason, some Minute Books are duplicated (when the rough minutes chance still to be extant) but this is not so in the present case.

To the simple structure of Weekly—Monthly—Quarterly—Yearly Meetings there were certain later developments. The question of separate Monthly Meetings for women was discussed in 1675 (8th and 9th Months) but nothing seems to have come of it, and the subject was raised again in 1689 (1st and 2nd Months) and the Women's Monthly Meeting was established 11 : v : 1690

[1] See Appendix under year 1667.

in this area.[1] In 1701 (2nd Month) and 1708 (4th Month and onwards) the Particular Meetings were advised to hold Preparative Meetings to sift the business in readiness for Monthly Meeting, and to keep Preparative Meeting Minutes. These, together with the Minutes of the Women's Meetings, form parallel series with those of the Men's Monthly Meeting and, occasionally, amplify some detail or elucidate an obscurity but, in general, they tend to be less informative, and Preparative Meeting Minutes have not been so sedulously kept or preserved.

Nationally, Meeting for Sufferings, the name of which is a sufficient indication of its original function, was instituted in 1676, William Garland, of Gainsborough, being the first Lincolnshire representative, and it became the standing executive committee of Yearly Meeting, in which capacity it exists to-day.

The Quarterly Meeting Minutes begin in the 1st Month of 1668, and at the second Meeting in the 4th Month, Monthly Meetings were instructed " 2dly That every Monthly Meeting Buy a Large Convenient Booke for Registring Births Marriages & Burialls, which have been amongst friends since they were a people, And that two faithfull friends of every perticular Meeting may be appointed to see it done by the Monthly Meeting, And what else is Remarkable to be recorded in that Meeting " so this is evidently the date at which the Registers were first introduced and the retrospective entries made.

At the 7th Month 1668 Quarterly Meeting it was " judged expedient & also very necessary that Friends belonging to the Severall private Meetings of this County do their utmost endeavours to procure the Setlement of Burying places that they may Remaine Certaine to Posterity, that they may not depend upon the will (of) one, but setled to Friends of the whole Meeting ". The first acquisition of real property in Gainsborough Monthly Meeting was the burial ground at Kexby where " Prudence, wife of Thomas Fisher 5th Month 1665 " had been buried, and he conveyed the small piece of land in November 1668. Many of Friends' burial grounds came in the same way, that is, by use as a private grave yard by the members of one family at first, and later conveyed for the use of Friends generally in that area.

Disputes between Quakers, which ordinarily would have been settled by legal process, had to be submitted to arbitration, the arbitrators being usually appointed by the Monthly Meeting. The prohibition of seeking legal redress, however, did not prevent a Quaker taking action against a Non-Friend, and if one party to a dispute refused to submit to arbitration or to accept the award of the arbitrators, Monthly Meeting was quite prepared to disown the recalcitrant and thus leave the other at liberty to sue at law if he chose.

[1] The Gainsborough Women's Monthly Meeting Minutes begin 12 : v : 1695.

As we have seen, the Quarterly Meeting kept Minutes from the beginning, and in the 7th Month of 1669 there appears " Let every Monthly Meeting take care that a booke be provided for every Monthly Meeting wherein what is done at every Monthly Meeting be Recorded ". Evidently Gainsborough Monthly Meeting complied quite quickly, for the Minutes start 12th Month 1669. One of the earliest entries in the Minute Book is a summary, under 10 headings, of the functions of a Monthly Meeting. Items 1–3 deal with poor relief, 4–6 with apostasy and discipline, 7 business arising from previous minutes, 8 with Births, Marriages and Burials, 9 with " Sufferings " and 10, primarily, with real property.

Quaker poor relief has always acted on the principle of putting the recipient into a better position to help himself, by such means as procuring accommodation or work, though many cases of widows or elderly people occur where pecuniary assistance was the only practical course and orphans were boarded out in Quaker homes until they were old enough to be apprenticed. Just as, under the Elizabethan Poor Law, the unit responsible for its own poor relief was the parish, so the corresponding Quaker unit was the Monthly Meeting. This practice of maintaining their own poor obviously needed some means of determining who was thus entitled to relief and this is the significance of the enquiry[1] as to whether a Friend who had removed to another area was " in unitie ". Ultimately, the present system of formal membership[2] and certification, on removal, from the Monthly Meeting of origin to that of destination was developed.

A special aspect of poor relief constantly recurs in the payment of funeral expenses.[3] Friends would be compelled to meet these charges when the interment was in accordance with their practice; if the parish paid the cost, the rites of the Established Church would have to be used.

To avoid the inhumanity of confining a lunatic in the local gaol, as was customary at that time, a Monthly Meeting would, if necessary, provide for the care of any one becoming mentally afflicted in their own home.[4] The case from Lea[5] where no such provision was made seems, therefore, to need some explanation, which may, perhaps, be found in the following entries taken from the Lea Parish Register :—

" 1695 Thomas the son of Thomas Rickitt & Susan his wife was baptised.

1696 Edward the son of Thomas Rickitt & Susanna his wife was baptized."

[1] See text under date 9 : xi : 1708.
[2] Rules adopted in 1737 by Yearly Meeting.
[3] See text under date 19 : x : 1681.
[4] Broughton Monthly Meeting Minutes under date 5 : 2 : 1688.
[5] See text under date 14 : xii : 1695 and later.

Such evidence of conformity would be an effective bar to eleemosynary or other assistance from Monthly Meeting, though the Women's Meeting did relieve the wife and children.[1]

A growing movement was bound to attract a certain proportion of weaker adherents who either could not withstand the pressure of persecution or maintain the high standard of conduct postulated by the "Inner Light". Matthew xviii, 15–17, is the basis of the disciplinary measures for such backsliders; private remonstrance, followed by reprobation by Monthly Meeting and the ultimate sanction of disownment, though, to avoid this, efforts were made to persuade the offender to make written acknowledgment of his offence (testify against himself). The instrument formally separating the individual from fellowship was, originally, a minute duly recorded but, later, a separate document called a "Testimony of Denial (or Disownment)" would be issued and, after a copy had been served on the offender, it was read at the Meeting he had attended and, usually but not invariably, copied into the Minute Book.

The more usual causes of disownment were: moral offences such as drunkenness, adultery, theft, etc., lack of business rectitude, apostacy, and marriage, either by a priest or with a non-quaker (i.e., Marriage out of the Society). Disownments for this last cause were so numerous during the 18th and early 19th centuries as to be a severe drain on the membership, in all probability the losses by "marrying-out" were greater than by death.

Other early entries relating to wills of deceased Friends may be due to a nebulous idea that, since they were setting up an organisation to replace that of the established Church and, as Probate was a function of the Ecclesiastical Courts, therefore, to provide full parallel facilities, they must take cognisance of testamentary documents. But, since no religious principle was involved, this practice could not form the basis of an enduring testimony and, sooner or later, all Monthly Meetings ceased to record wills. For Lincolnshire, Quarterly Meeting settled the matter by minuting that only wills in which Friends were nominated as trustees need be recorded. This was in 1679 and there are no later wills entered in the Gainsborough Minutes, but Kendal Monthly Meeting continued to record Westmorland Friends' wills until 1738.

Friends were interested in education from the first; when necessary, in boarding out orphans, Monthly Meeting stipulated that they should attend school[2] and Brigg Meeting attempted to found a school for themselves[3] but apparently could not provide sufficient financial backing and the schoolmaster removed to Gainsborough.

[1] Gainsborough Women's Monthly Meeting Minutes under date 13 : 2 : 1697.
[2] See text under date 12 : vii : 1690.
[3] *Ibid.* under date 13 : viii : 1705 *et seq.*

But, for the young, almost universal use was made of apprenticeship; there are many instances recorded when Monthly Meeting paid the premiums but these are a mere fraction of the total, for most Quakers were able to meet the cost themselves and so there would be no record in the minutes. A noteworthy feature was the trial period[1] ("alikeing") before the indentures were sealed. If the apprentice did not settle happily, Monthly Meeting would try to find another master; equally if the employer thought the child unsuitable[2] other arrangements would be made and this practice must have gone a long way towards avoiding misfits. Inevitably, there were some failures, as in the case of a runaway apprentice[3] who afterwards turned out to be an incorrigible rover. For adults, the provision and circulation of books was the normal educational method[4] leading to the formation of Meeting House libraries[5] which are almost universal to this day.

Prior to the Toleration Act, real property was, necessarily, almost confined to Burial Grounds, but as Meeting Houses were erected, and bequests received, repairs, renewals of trust and general property management provided an increasing volume of business. Toleration was soon followed by the erection of a Meeting House in Lincoln for the use of Quarterly Meeting[6] and apparently some premises in Brigg must have been adapted as a Meeting House by the following year.[7] Possibly similar adaptations took place at Winteringham,[8] West Butterwick[9] and Thealby,[10] but Gainsborough (1704) and Beltoft (1705) Meeting Houses were new from the ground.

The financing of these ventures varied somewhat; the cost of Lincoln Meeting House was shared out over the county, Brigg and Beltoft were assisted by Monthly Meeting with legacies which were at its disposal, but Gainsborough Friends subscribed the whole cost of their premises among themselves. Perhaps these variations reflect the relative prosperity of the different groups of Friends. All these Meeting Houses would need licensing, as would the private houses previously used; we cannot locate the earliest licences taken out because there are gaps in the Lindsey Quarter Sessions Rolls (1660–1700) and Minutes (1679–1703), but the Monthly Meeting Minute Book itself provides some information[11] and the original licences for Gainsborough and Beltoft are still extant while an attested copy dated 21 : x : 1706 is at Lincoln.

To study the progress of the movement, Yearly Meeting of 1682 addressed a series of three queries to the representatives of Quarterly Meetings: expanded to eight in 1696 (and more later) this questionnaire was regularly answered in writing by Monthly Meetings until

[1] See text under date 14 : v : 1688.
[2] *Ibid.* under date 9 : x : 1698.
[3] *Ibid.* under date 13 : v : 1681.
[4] *Ibid.* under date 8 : xi : 1691.
[5] *Ibid.* under date 12 : xii : 1691.
[6] *Ibid.* under date 11 : viii : 1689.
[7] *Ibid.* 12 : x : 1690.
[8] *Ibid.* under date 8 : iii : 1696.
[9] *Ibid.* under date 9 : v : 1697.
[10] *Ibid.* under date 10 : iii : 1700.
[11] *Ibid.* under date 14 : vii : 1698 and 7 : iv : 1706.

late in the 19th century. In many instances copies of these replies can be found in the minutes of Preparative Meetings, Monthly Meetings[1] and Quarterly Meetings, and comparison of sets of replies for given dates shows that it was a " boiling-down " process, each superior meeting summarising and grouping the information it received from its constituent meetings.

Though the routine tended to monotony, there is no doubt that this practice of regular, critical self-examination helped the society to maintain a high level of ethical behaviour during a period when the standard of morality in the world around was deplorably low.

Further steps in the same direction were the appointment of Overseers, to carry out the discipline[2] and the recording of the names of representatives[3] to disclose slackness in attendance at Monthly Meeting.

In the absence of a list of Members it is difficult to give a precise estimate of the strength of the movement during the period covered by the Minute Book. The Religious Census of 1676[4] groups all forms of Non-Conformity together and since the *Speculum Dioceseos*[5] enumerates by families, and the return for the town of Gainsborough is somewhat doubtful, it is unsafe to calculate from them. In any case, it is probable that the peak period had already been passed by then and the best estimate that can be formed is that, at its strongest, Quaker adherents in this area were about 1 per cent. of the population. They tended, moreover, to form groups, whereas Abraham de la Pryme, at Broughton, was able to write : " Thank God I have but one family of these damned Hereticks in my parish ",[6] the Rev. Samuel Wesley, at Epworth, reported " That there are about 40 Quakers and above 70 Anabaptists that insult him everywhere ".[7]

The antagonism which Quakerism aroused was out of all proportion to its numerical strength, e.g., it is noteworthy that in their earliest period the efforts of the Society for the Propagation of Christian Knowledge and the Society for the Propagation of the Gospel were largely directed against Quakerism.

Certain peculiarities of Quaker parlance need interpretation to render them intelligible. Universal salvability, as a purely spiritual process with the consequent futility of outward observance, constituted, for the early Quakers, " the Truth " and so that term for the basic concept became synonymous with Quakerism. Their earliest preachers were the " First Publishers of Truth ",

[1] See text under date 16 : xi : 1718. [2] *Ibid.* under date 11 : i : 1698.
[3] *Ibid.* under date 8 : i : 1706 and onwards.
[4] *Lincolnshire Notes and Queries XVI*, No. 2, pp. 47–50.
[5] R.E.G. Cole (ed.), *Speculum Dioceseos Lincolniensis* (1705–1723), L.R.S. IV, Part I, Lincoln, 1913.
[6] *Diary of Abraham de la Pryme*, Surtees Society, LIV, Durham, 1870, p. 136.
[7] *The History of the S.P.C.K.*, 1698–1898, W. O. B. Allen & E. McClure, London, 1898, p. 88.

a subscription for Quaker purposes was collected for "the needs of Truth", a non-Quaker was "out of the Truth" or was "one of the world", the "good order of Truth" or "wholesome order of Friends" means Quaker procedure. "To have unity with" is to be in agreement with, "disorderly walking" means conduct not in accordance with the rules, a "concern" is a strong desire to do something under divine guidance, while "conduct and conversation" covers general behaviour. The days of the week and the months of the year are always given numerically because of Friends' objection to the names of heathen deities as usually used.

Between the times when the present Minute Book opens and closes a profound change had come over Quakerism: where persecution had merely stimulated the dynamic enthusiasm of the somewhat aggressive First Publishers of Truth, the concessions which their sufferings had wrung from the state and the growing prosperity which sobriety and honest dealing brought, effected a subtle softening influence. Where Quakers had been burning with missionary zeal they began to turn inwards upon themselves and to develop those customs of dress, speech and behaviour which were to mark them out as a "Peculiar People". In this atmosphere the influence of Quietism readily took hold and a century or more was to pass before the Society of Friends began to shake off the deadening effect. So, although Quietism implies neither somnolence nor lethargy, a contemporary quotation from the mass of Anti-Quaker literature, in spite of the obviously exaggerated language, may typify the closing period thus: "An impediment their Hearers are now almost irrecoverably infected with; under a sorrowful sense whereof, one of their Preachers lately told us at Sleeford, that finding them almost all a Sleep in their Meeting at Gainsborough, amongst others he had visited, he was forc'd to clap his hands hard together, stamp his feet often upon his form and thrash them near two hours by the clock to awake them to hear him."[1]

[1] Henry Pickworth, *A Charge of Error, Heresy, etc.* London, 1716, p. 147.

1669

A Booke of Records for the Monthly Meeting on the North West parts of the County of Lyncolne wherein for the information of such as are concerned is Recorded severall things as well of Publique as of particular Concernment in Relaton to the pretious truth & those that make profession thereof. Here is allsoe Recorded seasonable admoniton & advise from severall Freinds of Truth to the Quarterly, Monthly & Weekly Meetings, wherein may be observed the Continuaton of Gods Loveing Kindness to Freinds in thus tenderly Vissitting, & alsoe Matter of great Incouragement to Freinds to persist in the way of Truth, being assured of the Lords owneing & assisting them in their faithfull walkeing in the same Truth wherein that wholesome admonition may be followed & the Love of God in some measure Answered by all the professors of the same Truth. Here is alsoe Recorded the Names of such as have beene convinced of the precious Truth who afterwards fell from the same, & became Scandalous in their Conversatons to the dishonour of Truth with the Vissitting of them againe by friends (in order to their Recovery by way of admoniton & Exhortaton & their Answers to Freinds & what since that tyme is become of them.

p. 2.

A Note of what things the Monthly Meetings ought to enquire of particular Meetings

1. First such Freinds as are poore be in any present necessity.
2. Whether there be any desolate widdows that stands in need of any advice or assistance.
3. Whether there be any orphans left to Freinds care.
4. Whether of those that were truly convinced & come once into the knowledge & obedience of the Truth, there be any lost in your Meeting.
5. Whether there be any that profess the precious Truth of God that have dishonoured it by goeing out into open profaneness of any kind.
6. Whether there be any that have beene spoken to for any private offence or wickednesse that refuse to heare & retorne.
7. Whether there be any accompt to be given of any thing that was refferred by the last Meeting.

8. Whether there be any marryage to publish or marryages, birthes or buryalls to be recorded.

9. What sufferings is there to record or xamples that have come upon persecutors.

10. Have you a burying place settled: and the Monthly Meeting is to see that nothing be lacking, that the lost be sought out; & that such as have dishonoured God be reproved & warned to repent: & such as justify any wickednesses; & are unruly be warned & that things that are to be recorded forthwith be done, but lett the Meeting beware of medling with particulars about trifles, but keepe in the weighty life, & sett the Truth above manifest wickednesse.

p. 3.

In the first month 69/70[1] William Dixon of Littlebrough in Nottinghamshire acquainted Freinds of the Monthly Meeting that he had intentions of marryage with Elizabeth Harpam (she being there present) of Gate Burton in the County of Lyncolne, the Monthly Meeting advised him to wayt theyr answer untill the Meeting following in the 2d month 70 that might have tyme to enquire whether they both was cleare from all others; & in the meane tyme they gave him a writeing under their hands to the Monthly Meeting in the County of Nottingham certyfying that he & she had beene att the Monthly Meetings to acquaint Freinds with such things & all things being cleare they knew nothing but they might joyne together in marryage which Monthly Meetings answer the said William Dixon was to bring with him in writeing under their hands to the Monthly Meeting which was to be in the second month 70[2] att Gainsborough.

It was expected att the Monthly Meeting in the 2d month abovesaid that William Dixon should have come to the Meeting to have had the answer of Freinds concerning his marryage; but he came not to the Meeting, it was therefore desired that Freinds of Gainsburgh Meeting should enquire concerneing him & bring an account the next Monthly Meeting.

p. 4.

Memorandum that the summe of five and forty pounds which was left unto Anne the Daughter of Thomas Hobson of Adlinfleet by the said Thomas her father as her filiall portion, and five pounds more left unto her by Anne Hobson her mother in law, is remaineing in the hand of Robert Ashton of Crowle for which he is accountable in time convenient.

Wittnes his own hand
the 8th day 3d month 1672[3] Robert Ashton

[1] March, 1670. [2] April, 1670. [3] 8th May, 1672.

Robert Ashton abovesaid hath acknowledged the receipt of the abovesaid sums of 45*l.* and 5*l.* in all fifty pounds and thereto subscribed as above the day & yeare above written in the presence of us witnesses.

more paid to Robt Ashton and Christopher Willson for the use of Anne Hobson

£	s.	d.
05 :	13 :	00

Joseph Richardson
William West
Edmund Morley
Christopher Willson
Robert Ruckhill
Richard Parnell
Thomas Wresle

Memorandum that the somme of five and twenty pounds which was left unto Sarah the daughter of the abovesaid Thomas Hobson by him her father as her filiall portion, and a cow given unto her by her mother sold for 3 pounds, in all eight & twenty pounds is remaining in the hand of me Christopher Willson senior of Adlinfleet for which I shall be accountable in time convenient.

witness my own hand subscribed

(8th May 1672) the 8th day, 3d month 1672 Christopher Willson

The receipt of the abovesaid sum of 28*l.* acknowledged and subscribed by the abovesaid Christopher Wilson the day & year abovesaid before us witnesses

Robert Ruckhill
Richard Parnell
William West
Robert Ashton
Edmund Morley
Joseph Richardson
Thomas Wresle

The abovesaid twenty eight pounds all discharged by the abovesaid Christopher Willson.

p. 5

Abraham Watson late of Butterwick by his will beareing date the 30 day of the eleaventh month called January 1667[1] gave these legacys following & did ordaine as followeth :—

first to his son John Watson he gives eight pounds to be paid unto him 25 day of the first month called March in the yeare 1668[2] to be paid to Thomas Wresle to put him to a trade.

item he gives to Margaret Tate & Ann Tate all his winter . . . . . . & one stacke of wheat.

item all the rest of his goods undisposed on he gives unto James Wattson his son whom he constitutes his sole executor &

[1] 30th January, 1668. [2] 25th March, 1668.

he ordered Thomas Browne of Buterwicke to have the tuition of James in his minority & the tenantship of his house he gives unto Thomas Browne for the bringing up of his son, & ordereth that the eight pounds given to his son John should be paid to Thomas Wresle of Butterwicke for the bringing him up & putting to a trade.

Witnesse Thomas Wresle Abraham Watson
Robert Cokes

The Inventory of the goods & chattells of the abovesaid Abraham Watson deceased. Praised by Thomas Maw, Thomas Wresle, Thomas Parkinson, Robert Cokes eight day of the month cald February 1667[1].

Imprimis his purse & apparell iii*l*. xiiii*s*.: gallow, balke, hooks & tongs ii*s*. vi*d*. all iii*l*. xvi*s*. vi*d*.

item 2 tables & 2 formes viii*s*.: chaires & stoles ii*s*. vi*d*.: one cupbord v*s*. all xv*s*. vi*d*.

item brasse & pewter & one iron pott x*s*.: wood & earth vessell iii*s*. iiii*d*. all xiii*s*. iiii*d*.

item Wright tooles iiii*s*. vi*d*.: 1 smothing iron xii*d*.: 1 kitt kimbling & other thing iiii*s*. vi*d*.

item 2 bedsteads & bedding iii*l*. xiii*s*.: for iii chests & lynings xxiii*s*. all iiii*l*. xvi*s*.

item For of all wood in the parlor ii*s*.: for pilld & brakd hempe iiii*l*. v*s*. all iiii*l*. vii*s*.

item for lyne drest & undrest iii*l*. iiii*s*.: syths spades & forks vi*s*.: all iii*l*. x*s*.

item for corne & hempeseed ii*l*. v*s*.: ii*l*. v*s*.

item for stocke brakes & wheelebarrow vi*s*.: vi*s*.

item 2 cows & fodder iii*l*.: turvs stocks & blocks xvi*s*. vi*d*.: iii*l*. xvi*s*. vi*d*.

item for sacks & pookes & things unmencond iii*s*. iiii*d*. iii*s*. iiii*d*.

debts owing to the deceased x*s*. x*s*.:

Some: xxv*l*.: viii*s*.: viii*d*.:

Thomas Browne of Butterwicke abovenamed did enter to the goods abovenamed according to the will of Abraham Wattson, wherewith he stands charged: since which tyme of his entry he hath paid as followeth:

Imprimis by monys owing to Thomas Parkinson paid by Thomas Browne ii*l*. ii*s*.:

paid more for hearth money & some other payments xii*s*.:

[1] 8th February, 1668.

paid to Thomas Wresle according to the will of A. W. viii*l*.: as a legacy to John Wattson his son:

This abovewritten taken out of the originall will & inventory of Abraham Wattson deceased & examined & agreeth with the same this wittnessed by

William Garland

The abovewritten account concerneing Abraham Wattson we doe hear confesse to witnesse our hands

his
Thomas T Browne
marke

Thomas Wresle

Friends in their Monthly Meeting the 14 day of the 11th month 1679[1] being satisfyed that the abovesaid Thomas Browne & Thomas Wresle have discharged the trust reposed in them by Abraham Watson as above written; have ordered their discharge to be recorded and it is hereby recorded, accordingly by

R. Rockhill

p. 6.

Att a Monthly Meeting 9: day of the 12th month 1669[2] held att Epworth for the North West parts of the County of Lyncolne:—

First it is concluded that the particular state & conditons of all such as have beene convinced of the precious truth & are growne careless & negligent in coming to Meetings or have any ways dishonoured Truth by their disorderly walkeing: may be brought in to the next Monthly Meeting, that it may appeare how farr Truth is cleare of them, & Freinds in their warneings, admonitions & exhortations to repentance.

2 It is concluded that the accounts of Thomas Browne & Thomas Wresle concerneing the will & inventory of Abraham Watson late of Butterwicke deceased be taken notice of the next Monthly Meeting that it may be recorded.

3 That generall contribution be maid throughout every particular Meeting & brought in to the next Monthly Meeting.

4 That as it is ordered that any are purposed to be joyned together in marryage that tymely care be taken to informe the parties of the order & way that is agreed upon by Freinds that nothing may be done in that weighty case but may be for the advancement of Truth, by the shutting out any disorderly practice which may tend to the gaineing of those that are without.

5 It is concluded the next Monthly Meeting be att Thomas Markeham att Brigg the case of John Marr, Susanna Browne & John Spicer referred to Quarterly Meeting.

[1] 14th January, 1680. 9th February, 1670.

A page concerneing paying of tithes to priests and impropriators.

Friends it was the testimony of the apostles and the primitive Christians and Saints against the types and all those figures and shaddows that were sett up by the commands of God, in the tyme of the law was held up by good men and soe Moses was read, and they that did despise Moses dyed under the hands of two or three witnesses, those that led people from the Law of God was to be stoned to death; through the mouths of wittnesses; and the witnesses hand must be upon them first: Now when Christ Jesus came as Moses prophesied of: Like unto me shall God raise up a prophett him shall you heare; soe Moses was nott to be heard, Moses bids nott heare him butt heare Christ the prophett, when he was raised up; who came to end all the figures and offerings and shaddows and the vailes and tithes of all sorts and soe all tyths were given since man fell into the earth and the types and figures and shaddows were given unto him since he fell, and as man comes up into the beginning, into the image of God, he comes out of the earth, out of types where he offered up tenths according to the Law: Soe that as there was noe tyths to be paid before the fall, soe noe Tyths to be payd of out of the fall as there was noe shaddows and figures given to man before the fall; Soe there is none to be observed as man comes up out of the fall by Christ Jesus, who ends all the figures and shaddows and takes away the vailes and ends the shaddows; now the Saints was against tyths which God had comanded and against those offerings, sacrifices which was the comand of God, sett up by God, and good men: Soe since the apostles days tyths and the offerings have been set up by such as have gone out of the power & Spirit the apostles was in: Which now is our testimony against the ordinance of men the rudiments of the world and doctrines and comands of men, which have beene sett up by men, their meintenance have beene sett up by men, since they lost the spirit and power the apostles were in; soe they that keep that testimony of Jesus that is the spirit the apostles were in, beares theyr testimony against; those things that they have sett up since the Apostles dayes, to witt tyths of all sorts, I say by the same spirit as the apostles bore their testimony against those tyths and offerings that God had comanded; Now if some say that the impropriators have bought the tyths: can any man sell another mans coate & he to take two or three by force for it, is this the spirit of Christ that doth so; is this the spirit that you have unity with: is not this the spirit that must be judged; being many have laid downe lives against it. And many Freinds that have tyths of their own, that were impropriators; when they came to be convinced of Truth; they denyed them and threw them up and would not receive them, therefore can any man pay them either to preists or impropriators did they not come all from one ground and is it nott knowne that if people did nott labor, and keepe servants; and sow and buy cattell the preist would gett as little upon the bare ground as the impropriator it is upon the labor of the servants and familys that they have tenths:

p. 8.

Att a Meeting held att Garthorpe in the third month 1670[1] it was concluded as followeth:—

First that generall contribution be maid throughout every Meeting belonging to the North West parts of this county & be brought in to the next Monthly Meeting & that care be taken that the necessities of Freinds who are soe indeed be brought up to the Monthly Meeting that the whole Meeting may consider of them, that from thence they may be supplyed.

It was ordered that the next Monthly Meeting be att Thomas Wresls att Butterwicke.

Att a Meeteing held att Butterwicke the 8th day of the 4th month 1670[2]: concluded as followeth:—

First that the next Monthly Meeteing be att Thomas Markhams house in Brigg.

And whereas Edward Farr of Gainsburgh, butcher, was reproved, exhorted & warned, by severall Freinds belonging to Gainsburgh Meeting, because of some misdemeanour charged against him, it was desired that he might appeare att the Quarterly Meeting held att Lyncolne for the whole county.

	£	s.	d.
The whole contributons brought as a free gift to the Monthly Meeting	05	10	08
The sum deducted to supply present necessity ..	01	18	06
The som carryed up to Lyncolne to the Quarterly Meeting	03	12	02

Thomas Wresle of Butterwicke acquainted Freinds that it was his purpose to take Mary Pane at Hawnby to wife, the said Mary & some of her freinds being then present, whereupon inquiry was to be maid concerning the clearness of them both from any other persons, this was the first tyme the thing was maid publicke.

Att a Monthly Meeting held the 13th of the fifth month cald July 1670[3]:—

Thomas Wresle came the second tyme to the Monthly Meeting to know the mind of Freinds concerining his maryage with he intended wife Mary Pane abovesaid; & Freinds there present declared that they had unity with the thing.

[1] May, 1670. [2] 8th June, 1670. [3] 13th July, 1670.

Certifyd the same to the Monthly Meeting of Mumby to which Monthly Meeting the said Mary did belong: it being manifest to Freinds that they both was cleare from all other persons:

It was then ordered that next Monthly Meeting should be att Robert Reeders att Temple Hall in Belton parish in the Ile of Axholme:

Att a Monthly Meeting held att Temple Hall in Belton parish in the Ile of Axholme the 10th day of the 6th month cald August 1670 concluded as followeth:—

First that generall contributons be maid throughout every Meeting in particular & brought in to the next Monthly Meeting.

That the next Monthly Meeting be the first fourth day of the 7th month 70[1]: att Elizabeth Barrows att Parke.

That Symon Rosse have the som of 5*s.*: to releive his present necessity.

That Freinds of Gainsburgh Meeting take care to releive Christopher Codd in his present necessity.

Att a Monthly Meeting held att Parke in the Ile of Axholme 7th day 7th month 1670[2]:

	£	s.	d.
Contributons from Gainsburgh ..	00	13	10
Haxey Contributon	00	12	00
Crowle Contributon..	00	14	03
Garthorpe Contributon	00	18	02
Winteringham Contributon ..	00	18	06
Brigg Contributon	00	16	00
Som:	04	12	09

	£	s.	d.
Returned backe to William Clarke..	00	06	00
Ordered that Gainsburgh Meeting have the som of to supply the necessities of Freinds withall & to give an account of the disbursement of it to the Monthly Meeting.	02	06	09
Ordered that the remainder of the contributon being be carryed up to the Quarterly Meeting 30th instant.	02	00	00

John Clam was accused of goeing into open profaneness fighting in an alehouse, it was desired by the Monthly Meeting that Freinds of Crowl Meeting should exhort & reproove him & bring his answer to the next Monthly Meeting.

[1] The first Wednesday in September, 1670. [2] 7th September, 1670.

Michajah Wake & Elizabeth Allen declared that they had a purpose to be joind together in marryage; they was desired to wait Freinds answer untill next Monthly Meeting.

Thomas Browne & Hanah Turner declared that they had a purpose to be joyned together in marryage, they was desired to wayt Freinds answer untill next Monthly Meeting:

Stephen Parr: declared together with Frances Warrener that they had a purpose to be joyned together in marryage; they was desired to wait Freinds answer untill next Monthly Meeting.

It is ordered that the next Monthly Meeting be att Butterwicke.

p. 10.

ATT a Monthly Meeting at Butterwick the 12th day of the 8th month 1670[1]:—

Michajah Wake & Thomas Brown, Stephen Parratt came the second time in to the Monthly Meeting to know the minde of Freinds concerning there respective marriages and Freinds did then and there declare there freedom in thing.

John Brown of West Butterwick came into the Monthly Meeting and there declared his intention to take Margret Tate to wife, she being present and declared her assent to the thing and Freinds have taken it in to consideration untill the next Monthly Meeting this being the first time the thing was made publick.

Freinds of Crowle Meeting are desired to admonish John Cam for his disorderly walking and to return his answer to the next Monthly Meeting.

It is ordered that the next Monthly Meeting be held att Thomas Markham house in Brigg.

ATT a Monthly Meeting held att Thomas Markehams house in Brigg: 9: day of the 9th month 1670[2]:—

John Cham of Butterwicke was admonished by Freinds of Crowle Meeting to that which did att first convince him, he declared to the clearing of Truth that the ground of his goeing out from Truth was only in himselfe, Stephen Parratt was desired to speake to him againe from the Monthly Meeting that if possible he may be regained to Truth:

It is ordered that generall contributons be maid throughout every Meeting of these parts of the County & be brought into the next Monthly Meeting & that Freinds att that Monthly Meeting signify the necessitys of Freinds that they may be supplyed.

[1] 12th October, 1670. [2] 9th November, 1670.

John Browne did againe acquaint Freinds of his intentions to take Margaret Tate to wife; Freinds declared theyr assent, that none had any thing against itt, this being the second tyme of makeing it Publicke:

It is ordered that the next Monthly Meeting be att the house of Richard Parnell of Epworth:

It is ordered that enquiry be maid whatt was the cause that Freinds of Garthorpe & Haxey had none for them appeared att the Monthly Meeting, there being as the Monthly Meeting judges an absolute necessity that some Freinds appeare from every Meeting. Haxey Meeting had one came though late:

p. 11.

Att a Monthly Meeteing held att the house of Richard Parnell in Epworth upon the 14th day of the 10th month 1670[1]:—

	£	s.	d.
The whole contributions brought as a free gift to the Monthly Meeteing	04	01	10½
deducted to supply present necessity	01	07	06
the sum to carry up to the Quarterly Meeting to Lincolne	02	14	04½

Stephen Parrat (as he was ordered by the last Monthly Meeteing) spooke to John Cham, but he the said Cham returned no answer.

Will Dixon of Littleborough in the county of Nottingham bringing a certificate from the Monthly Meeteing whereunto he belongs by which wee apprehending all things apperteineing thereto[2] cleare have consented to his marriage.

Itts ordered that the next Monthly Meeteing be held att the house of William Berrier in Crowle.

Att a Meeting held at the house of William Berrier in Crowle the 11th of 11th month 1670[3]:—

It is ordered by the Monthly Meeting that the weekly mainteinance of Christopher Codd be continued, & that Freinds of Gainsbrough Meeting take care therof.

	£	s.	d.
Memorandum that the sum of 17*s.* was sent from the Monthly Meeting to Gainsbrough Meeting for the payment of the halfe years rent of the abovesaid Christopher Codd	00	17	00

Memorandum it was taken into consideration as concerning providein a house for William Lambert, & was thought meet to leave it to the next Monthly Meeting.

[1] 14th December, 1670. [2] *Sic;* are *omitted.* [3] 11th January, 1671.

It is ordered that the next Monthly Meeting be at Robert Reeders house in Belton, viz. Temple Hall.

p. 12.

Att a Monthly Meeting held att Robt Reeders att Belton the 8th day of the 12th month 1670[1] :—

It is ordered that Freinds belonging to Gainsburgh Meeting take care to helpe William Lambert to provide him a house, & this Monthly Meeting is to have them indemnified.

It is ordered that an exact account of all sufferings that yett unbrought up ; be brought in with the day, place, sufferers, persecutor, name, to the next Monthly Meeting, to the end that they may be recorded & what examples have come upon persecutors.

It is ordered that a generall contribution be maid throughout every Meeting belonging to this Monthly Meeting & brought in to the next Monthly Meeting & that Freinds take care to give tymely notice of the same.

John Cham a Man formerly convinced of Truth turned away from it into open profaneness hath beene admonished to repent & retorne yett notwithstanding, continues in his wickedness, it is desired that if any Freinds have freedom, or see any thing further, as to speake to him againe that if possible he may retorne to Truth againe :

It is ordered that the next Monthly Meeting be att the house of Thomas Markeham att Brigg :

Att a Monthly Meeting held at Brigge the 8th day of the first month 70/71[2] at the house of T. Markham :—

John Odlin of Glamford Briggs came into the Monthly Meeting and there declared his intentions to take Sarah Ruckhill to wife, shee being there present and also declared her assent, and have submitted it to the consideration of Friends till the next Monthly Meeting.

At the meeting abovesaid the case of Matthew Tranmore of Luddington was layd before Friends who doe all with one consent advise him to mannage his business with wisdom & discression & in noe wise to fly his country & doe reffer the further consideration of his unjust vexaton to the next Quarterly Meeting.

The next Monthly Meeting to be at the house of John Dent, Thealby.

[1] 8th February, 1671. [2] 8th March, 1671.

p. 13.

At a Monthly Meeting of Friends held at Thealby at the house of John Dent the 12th day of the second month 1671[1] :—

It is ordered that the sume of 18*s.* 6*d.* sent from the Quarterly Meeting be sent back to Gainsburgh Meeting that Friends there may supply the present necessity of Christopher Codd and other indigent Friends according to their needs respectively, and that the finall settlement of their weekly supply be referred to the determination of the next Monthly Meeting, also, in regard a cleare account of Friends sufferings about Epworth could not be had at present, the disposure of the moneys sent from Friends for the reliefe of such sufferers is referred to the next Monthly Meeting also.

John Odlin of Glamford Briggs appeared the 2d time before Friends and further acquainted them with his purpose to take Sarah Ruckhill to wife, and Friends there unanimously declared their approbation & consent to the thing, so that they may have freedome to proceed at their own convenience.

It is ordered that the next Monthly Meeting be held at the house of Thomas Wresle of West Butterwicke.

William Lambert of Somerby deceased maid a bill of sale to William Garland & Henry Simpson both of Gainsburgh in the 2d month 1671[2] : of all his estate whatt soever for & towards the bringing up of his daughter Mary an infant aged about 5 quarters of yeare. William Garland in the absence of Henry Sympson tooke possession of the goods which was supposed to be worth about 19*l.* : for which hee will give an account to Freinds upon required, the child is now att the charge of the said William Garland upon the account above said taken care for this subscribed

by William Garland

Att a Monthly Meeting held att Thomas Wresles of Butterwicke the 10th day of the 3d month 1671[3] :—

It is ordered that the necessity of Freinds belonging to Gainsburgh as Christopher Codd & John Hooton be supplyed att the discretion of Gainsburgh Meeting, & they to give an account the next Monthly Meeting. Freinds takeing account of the Monys that came from London for the sufferers upon the account of the Act, it was found that there was a want of 3*s.* & 6*d.* which was supposed was sent to Mumby Meeting in regard they had 3*s.* : 8*d.* & ought to have butt 3*s.* 1½*d.* It is ordered that the disposure of it be refered to the next Monthly Meeting

[1] 12th April, 1671. [2] April, 1671. [3] 10th May, 1671.

& that the Monthly Meeting signify the same to the Mumby Freinds, to the intent they may restore theyr overplus where tis wanting.

It is ordered that the next Monthly be att the house of Thomas Markeham att Brigg.

p. 14.

At a Monthly Meeting held at the house of Thomas Markham of Glamford Briggs the 14th day of the 4d month 1671[1] :—

	£	s.	d.
From Gainsburgh	00	17	04
Wintringham	00	18	09
Brigge	00	12	00
Epworth	00	08	00
Crowle..	00	15	08
Adlinfleet	00	12	06
	04	04	03

	£	s.	d.
Sent back to W. G. as due to him	01	09	03
to Garthrope for supply of the necessity of widdow Goodall	00	05	00
to Crowle for the necessityes of Symon Ross ..	00	02	06
to Brigg for supply of widow Rogers her necessityes	00	02	06
to Epworth for supply of 2 poore Freinds there ..	00	08	00
To be sent to Lincoln to the Quarterly Meeting ..	01	00	00

At a Monthly Meeting held at the house of Thomas Markham of Glamford Briggs the 14th day of the 4th month 1671[2] :—

John Wresle of Thealby came into the Meeting and there declared his purpose to take Elizabeth Johnson to wife shee being there present and also declared her assent and have submitted their said purpose to the consideration of Freinds untill the next Monthly Meeting.

At the same time also Abraham Northen of Gate Burton came into the said Meeting and there declared his intentions to take Elizabeth Wood of Eagle to wife, shee being alsoe there present and declared her assent, and have submitted their said purpose to the consideration of Friends untill the next Monthly Meeting.

The next Monthly Meeting appointed to be at the house of Henry Symson of Gainsburgh.

[1] 14th June, 1671. [2] 14th June, 1671.

p. 15.

Att a Monthly Meeting the 12th day of the 5th month 1671[1]: held att the house of Henry Sympson of Gainsburgh :—

	£	s.	d.
Paid to Thomas Wresle to supply the necessity of Jane Carnell	00 :	02 :	06

John Wresle of Thealby came into the Meeting & declared a second tyme that he had a purpose to take Elizabeth Johnson to wife, butt she nott being there present it was refferred to Winteringham Meeting to give theire consents if all things be cleare on both sides.

Abraham Northerne of Gate Burton came a second tyme into the Meeting & declared his purpose to take Elizabeth Wood to wife she being there present, & in regard the father of the said Elizabeth hath beene unwilling, it is referred to Gainsburgh Meeting to enquire into it, & give an account to the North Clay Monthly Meeting that Truth may be cleare & nott be brought to suffer.

The next Monthly Meeting appointed to be att Robt Reeders att Belton :

Anthony Turner of Gainsburgh Meeting acquainted Freinds with his intentons to take Ann Pheasant to wife she being there present, & Freinds of the Monthly Meeting desired them to wayt a tyme that enquiry might be maid if all things were cleare on both sides.

Att a Monthly Meeting the 9th 6th month 1671[2] held at the house of Robert Reeder at Temple hall then

There Thomas Markham declared his intentions to take Jane Popple to wife and left it to Freinds to consider of untill the next Monthly Meeting.

It is ordered that contributions be collected in the severall Meetings, and brought to the next Monthly Meeting.

The next Monthly Meeting is appoynted at Thomas Wresle his house in West Butterwick.

Books to Freinds 14 : 12 : 71

Winteringham Robert Wilkinson ..	03 : 00
Brigg Edward Gilliatt	04 : 00
Robert Ruckhill	03 : 06
Robert Reeder	04 : 02

[1] 12th July, 1671. [2] 9th August, 1671.

p. 16.

ATT a Monthly Meeting held att Thomas Wresle his house att Butterwicke 13th day of September 1671[1] :—

		£	s.	d.
Contributions	from Gainsburgh Meeting	00 :	15 :	06
	from Epworth	00 :	08 :	04
	from Crowle	00 :	18 :	00
	from Winteringham..	00 :	16 :	09
	from Brigg	00 :	15 :	00
	from Garthorpe	00 :	14 :	00
Given Thomas Markham that he laid out		00 :	10 :	00
To William Garland that he disbursed		00 :	03 :	00
More to William Garland left in his hands ..		00 :	14 :	00

Ordered that the som of 3*l*. be sent to the Quarterly Meeting to be disposed on there as Freinds may see meet.

Thomas Markham againe acquainted Freinds that it was his intentons to take Jane Pople of Dyon house in the parish of Henbrough in Yorkshire to wife & did bring a certificate that he had done the same in the Monthly Meeting to which she did belong two severall tymes & Freinds did declare their sattisfaction as to his cleareness from any other woeman soe the thing was left to Freinds in Yorkshire & themselves to perfect.

Anthony Turner & Ann Pheasant did againe come to the Monthly Meeting & acquaint Freinds with their intentions of marryage & things being cleare on both their parts it was left to the consideraton of Freinds at Gainsburgh Meeting to see that care be taken by them to secure something for her children.

John Barrow of Haxey & Alce Tate of the same came into the Meeting & acquainted Freinds with their intentons of marryage & the thing was left to the consideration of Freinds untill the next Monthly Meeting.

The next Monthly Meeting is appointed att Elizabeth Barrows att Parke :

Bookes : To Epworth 40 sheets John Urry
To Winteringham : 54½ Anthony Westaby received for these
To Garthorpe 63½ Mathew Tranmore
To Butterwicke Thomas Wresle 1 booke : 16*d.*
To Brigg 49½ Thomas Markham

[1] 13th September, 1671.

p. 17.

ATT a Meeting held att Elizabeth Barrows house in Parke 11th day of 8ber 1671[1]:—

	£	s.	d.
Ordered by this Meeting that An Sampson of Lownd have towards the relief of her necessity	00 :	05 :	00
The same tyme to two poore Freinds in Crowle Meeting	00 :	04 :	00

John Barrow & Alce Tate came a second tyme into the Meeting & acquainted Freinds with theyr intentons of marryage & all things being cleare they was left to theyr freedomes to perform the same att tyme convenient.

The next Monthly Meeting ordered to be att Thomas Markhams house in Brigg.

AT a Monthly Meeting of Friends held at the house of Thomas Markham of Glamford Brigg the 8th day of the 9th month 1671[2]:—

William Hewit of Glentworth and Frances Hutton of the same came before Friends and there declared their intentions to joyne together in marriage, and are desired to waite the answer of Friends at the next Monthly Meeting.

Whereas James Dixon of Crowle hath appeared the last Monthly Meeting at the Parke the 11th day October and there published his intentions of marriage with Penelope Woollard of Aughton and hath come before Friends the second time at a Monthly Meeting held at the house of Thomas Markham at Brigg this present 8th day 9th month haveing brought with him a certificate from Friends of the Monthly Meeting of York (where the said Penelope dwelleth) wherein Friends there doe certify that all things on the woemans part are cleare and wee of this Monthly Meeting have certifyed the Friends of York Meeting of the proceedings here and that all things are clear also on the man's part therefore they are left to their liberty to proceed according to the wholesome order of Friends in that behalfe provided when they shall have time convenient.

The next Monthly Meeting to be held at Boterwick at the house of Thomas Wresle.

p. 18.

ATT a Monthly Meeting held att Butterwicke the 10 day of the xth month 1671[3]:—

The case of Joseph Cooper of Haxey who was marryed by a priest was brought before Freinds & it was by the Meeting desired that Christopher Edwards John Ury, & Robert Everatt should

[1] 11th October, 1671. [2] 8th November, 1671. [3] 10th December, 1671.

speake to him, to reproove him for soe doeing & to exhort him to that by which he was att first vissitted that if possible he may be recovered to Truth againe & that they alsoe speake to Adam Pilsworth & William Emly who have severall wayes dishoned[1] Truth & bring theyr answer to the next Monthly Meeting.

Contributons brought in	£	s.	d.
from Gainsburgh	00	15	02
Crowl	00	13	05½
Garthorpe	00	13	01
Winteringham	00	18	00
Brigg	00	15	00
Epworth	00	09	08
	04	04	04
Retornd backe to Winteringham	00	04	04
Retornd to Crowle	00	04	00
To Gainsburgh: to William Garland	00	13	06
That was laid out	00	02	06
	01	04	04
The remainder ordered to be sent to Lyncolne	03	00	00

William Hewett & Frances Hudson came a second tyme into the Meeting & declared it was their intents to be joyned together in marryage, & they being cleare in the Judgement of Freinds from all other persons they was left to theyr owne freedoms to perfect the same when they saw convenient:

It is desired that the Monthly Meeting may consider Robert Ruckhills case & paynes in writeing & keeping the record.

It is ordered that the next Monthly Meeting be att Robert Ashtons att Crowle.

Thomas Scarbrough of Ferryby & Ellen Brooke of Elsam came into the Meeting & declared theyr intentes as to marryage, & they was desired to wayt Freinds answer the next Monthly Meeting.

p. 19.

At a Monthly Meeting of Friends held at the house of Robert Ashton at Crowle the tenth day of the eleventh month 1671[2]:—

According to the desire of Friends the last Monthly Meeting Christopher Edwards John Urye & Robert Everat have gone to Joseph Cooper & William Emley to reproove & admonish

[1] *Sic: recte* dishonoured. [2] 10th January, 1672.

them &c. William Emley acknowledging his runing out from the truth and owning condemnation for the same & hath given hopes to Friends of his return to the Truth, but forasmuch as the answer of Joseph Cooper was not satisfactory, the same Friends (or any other who have freedome to it) are againe desired to visit Joseph Cooper, & Adam Pilsworth and further admonish them that they may be senseable of their offences, and return unfainedly to the unity of Friends in the Truth.

	£ s. d.
Distributed of the mony that came from the Quarterly Meeting unto John Pilsworth of Epworth the sum of	01 : 00 : 00
distributed unto John Clarke of Haxey the sum of..	01 : 00 : 00
As for other Sufferers (a true account not being had of the full of their sufferings) their case is referred to a further opportunity.	
Sent to Gainsburgh Meeting the sum of	00 : 10 : 00
Remaines yet undisposed the sum of	02 : 10 : 00

Thomas Scarbrough of Ferriby & Helene Brooke of Elsham have made noe appearance at this Meeting.

The next Meeting to be held at the house of Thomas Markham in Glamford Briggs.

Att a Monthly Meeting held at the house of Thomas Markham att Brigg: 14th day of the 12th month 1671[1]:—

It is ordered that generall contribution be maid throughout every Meeting on the North West parts of the County of Lyncolne & brought in to the next Monthly Meeting, or Quarterly Meeting, which shall first happen & there disposed on as Freinds may see meet for the service of Truth.

It is ordered that Thomas Wresle & Christopher Edwards doe againe vissitt William Emley, Joseph Cooper & Adam Pilsworth & as they may feele the Truth arise in theyr hearts to exhort, admonish or reprove them, as they may be made sensible of their severall conditins, & bring their answers to the next Monthly Meeting.

Sent Thomas Read of the monys above: 10*s*: reste 40*s*:

Given to Robert Reeder for the necessity of Symon Ross of Belton 00 : 02 : 06.

Thomas Scarbrough of Ferriby & Ellen Brooke of Elsham came a second tyme into the Meeting, & acquainted Friends with their intentons of marryage, it was then ordered that Freinds of

[1] 14th February, 1672.

Brigg Meeting take care the portions of the children of Ellen Brooke be secured, which being done it is left to theyr discretions to consumate the thing as they see meet according to the wholesome order of Truth.

The next Monthly Meeting appointed att Christopher Edwards house in Epworth.

p. 20.

At a Monthly Meeting of Friends held at the house of Christopher Edwards in Epworth the thirteenth day of the first month 1671/2[1] :—

Thomas Wresle & Christopher Edwards have again visited William Emley & Joseph Cooper (according to the desire of Friends) and doe report that they found Joseph Cooper meek and low in his mind and loving to Friends that did visit him takeing their visit in love, expressing to them his hopes that all would be well in time, and that he hoped to overcome such things as at present were impediments unto him, acknowledging himself more sensible of his miscarriage in the thing imputed as a fault unto him, then he was before.

And they report of William Emley that his behaviour was very high, too much savouring of scornfulness, & derision wondring why Friends would soe needlesly trouble themselves about him, desireing to be let alone, as a man resolved what to doe, beareing himselfe (indeed) as if he were above all reproofe.

Contributons brought in	£	s.	d.
from Gainsbrough Meeting	00 :	16 :	04
from Crowle Meeting	00 :	12 :	04
from Brigg Meeting	00 :	18 :	00
from Wintringham Meeting	00 :	18 :	02
from Garthrope Meeting	00 :	12 :	10
	03 :	17 :	08
Sent back to the poor of Brigg Meeting.. ..	00 :	02 :	06
to the poor of Crowle Meeting ..	00 :	04 :	00
To Gainsbrough Meeting	00 :	11 :	02
In W. Garlands hand before	00 :	09 :	07
To be sent up to the Quarterly Meeting	03 :	0 :	00

The next Meeting to be at the house of Henry Sympson in Gainsburgh.

The next Monthly Meeting is to be at the house of Christopher Wilsons in Adlinfleet.

[1] 13th March, 1672.

p. 21.

At a Monthly Meeting of Friends held at the house of Christopher Willson of Adlinfleet the eighth day of the 3d month 1672[1] :—

It is desired by Friends that Joseph Cooper of Epworth be once againe visited and admonished to returne to the truth from which he hath made defection & Edmond Morley & Robert Ruckhill are desired to accept of the said service and to make report of his answer the next Monthly Meeting.

Ordered that the fourty shillings which was left in Thomas Markhams hand and the ten shillings formerly in William Garlands be forthwith payd unto Christopher Edwards of Epworth.

Ordered also that a contribution be brought in the next Monthly Meeting which is appointed to be at the house of William Harrison in Winteringham.

At a Monthly Meeting of Friends held at the house of William Harrison of Winteringham the twelth day of the fourth month 1672[2] :—

Contributons brought in	£	s.	d.
from Gainsbrough Meeting	1 :	3 :	9
from Crowle Meeting	0 :	15 :	2
from Brigg Meeting	0 :	17 :	4
from Winteringham	0 :	16 :	6
from Garthorpe Meeting	0 :	15 :	0
from Epworth Meeting	0 :	13 :	0
	5 :	0 :	9

The fourty shillings in Thomas Markhams hand hath been payd by him according to the abovesaid order.

Given to Garthorpe Meeting for the poore .. .. 0 : 5 : 0

This Monthly Meeting refers the care of Christophers Cods children to Friends of Gainsbrough Meeting.

Sent to Will Garland upon the account of prisoners which he hath laid out of purss 9*s*.

p. 22.

That whereas Robert Ruckhill & Edmond Morley was desired the last Monthly Meeting to goe to speak to Joseph Cooper of Haxey to return to the Truth but have not brought in there answer to this Monthly Meeting.

William West of Willingham & Elizabeth Northen of Gate Burton came into the Meetting & acquainted Freinds with their intentions of marriage, & the thing was left to the consideration of Freinds till the next Monthly Meetting.

[1] 8th May, 1672. [2] 12th June, 1672.

	£ s. d.
To be sent to the Quarterly Meetting	04 : 06 : 9

The next Monthly Meeting is ordered to be at Crowle at Robert Ashtons.

Att a Monthly Meeting held at Crowle att the house of Robert Ashton the 10th day of the fift month 1672[1] :—

Robert Ruckhill & Edmond Morley are still desired by this Meeting to vissitt Joseph Cooper, in order to the regaining him to the Truth & bring in his answer next Monthly Meeting.

William West & Elizabeth Northen came a second tyme into the Meeting to acquaint Freinds with theyr intenton of marryage & nothing appeareing butt that all things was cleare on both sides, it was left to themselves to apoint a Meeting by the advice of Freinds of Gainsburgh Meeting to consumate the same.

It is ordered that the next Monthly Meeting be att the house of Richard Parnell of Epworth.

p. 23

At a Monthly Meeting of Friends held at the house of Richard Parnell of Epworth the fourteenth day of the sixth month 1672[2] :—

Edmund Morley & Robert Ruckhill have been again to visit Joseph Cooper and doe give the same account of him as Friends formerly upon the like service have done & not otherwise.

	£ s. d.
Disbursed unto Symon Rosse of Belton for the supply of his present nesessity out of the contributons the sum of	00 : 03 : 04

Ordered that a contribution be gathered & brought in to the next Monthly Meeting which is appointed to be at the house of Thomas Markham of Glamford Briggs.

At a Monthly Meeting of Friends held at the house of Thomas Markham at Glamford Briggs the 11th day of the 7th month 1672[3] :—

Contributions brought in	£ s. d.
Brigg	01 : 01 : 06
from Crowle	00 : 19 : 02
Garthrope	00 : 13 : 04
Wintringham	00 : 18 : 01
Gainsburgh	01 : 13 : 05
Epworth	00 : 10 : 04
	05 : 15 : 10

[1] 10th July, 1672. [2] 14th August, 1672. [3] 11th September, 1672.

	£	s.	d.
Returned back for the supply of poor Friends			
To Garthrope Meeting	00	05	00
To Crowle Meeting	00	05	00
To Gainsburgh Meeting	01	05	10
to be sent to the Quarterly Meeting	04	00	00
Remaining in the hand of William Garland of his last account the sume of	00	04	07

The next Meeting is appointed at the house of Henry Sympson in Gainsburgh.

p. 24

At a Monthly Meeting of Friends held at the house of Henry Sympson in Gainsburgh the 9th day of the 8th month 1672.[1]

The present determination of Friends concerning the children of Charles Tate deceased is that the boy be left to the disposing of Friends of Epworth Meeting and that they give account what they shall doe concerning him at the next Monthly Meeting and further that the girle be disposed of unto John Browne of Boterwicke untill such time as Friends of the Monthly Meeting can otherwise provide for her and to have according to the rate of forty shillings by the year allowed proportionably for her keeping untill she be otherwise disposed of in the mean time to be reasonably apparrelld at the charge of Frends.

It is further concluded & agreed by Friends of the Monthly Meeting that Rebekah the daughter of Christopher Codd deceased be disposed of unto William West of Gate Burton in the manner of an Apprentice for the terme of ten years from the first day of the third month 1672 and that there be payd unto the said William West in consideration of his keeping of the said Rebekah the summe of seaven pounds & ten shillings, the time & manner of payment to be left to the discresion of Friends of this Monthly Meeting.

The next Monthly Meeting to be at the house of Thomas Wressle at Boterwicke.

At a Monthly Meeting of Freinds held at the house of Thomas Wressle of Butterwick the 13 day of the 9th month 1672[2] :—

Itt was then ordered that a contribution be collected in every Monthly Meeting and brought up to the next Monthly Meeting.

It is ordered that the boy of Charles Tate deceased which was left to the disposing of Freinds of Epworth Meeting be disposed

[1] 9th October, 1672. [2] 13th November, 1672.

of accordingly and to give an account thereof to the next Monethly Meeting.

p. 25

It is further concluded that the disposing of Rebeckah the daughter of Christopher Codd deceased as also the payment of the money be left to the consideration of Freinds of the next Monethly Meeting.

	£ s. d.
Disposed of to the poore of Crowle Meeting	00 : 04 : 00

The next Monethly Meeting be held at Thomas Markham house in Brigg.

At a Monethly Meeting held at Thomas Markham his house in Brigg the 11th December 1672[1] :—

The case of Thomas Scarbrough & his wife was had under consideration & it was ordered that two Freinds of Brigg Meeting should admonish them to return to the Truth & give account of there answer to the next Monthly Meeting.

It is further concluded by this Monethly Meeting that William Garland and Thomas Wressle speak to Michael Monkton, Robert Everat & Peter Moody concerning Peter Moody his disorderly marriage & to give account of ther answers to the next Monethly Meeting.

The contribution sent up to Lincoln from the Monethly Meeting is	06 : 10 : 02

It is ordered that the next Monethly Meeting be at the house of Thomas Wresle in Butterwick.

Att a Monethly Meeting held at Thomas Markham his house in Brigg the 8th day 11th moneth 1672/3[2] :—

It is again desired that William Garland & Thomas Wressle speak to Robert Everat & Peter Moody concerning Peter Moody his disorderly marriag & give account of there answer to the next Monethly Meeting.

Thomas Markham & William Smith according to the order of the Monethly Meeting have spoaken to Thomas Scarbrough & Ellen his wife concerning their remissness in coming to Meeting as also the blott cast upon Truth by reason of them

p. 26

and there answer was, the reason wherefore they did not come to our Meeting as formerly was because they perceived a

[1] 11th December, 1672. [2] 8th January, 1673.

straitness in Freinds in regard they did lye under that reproach and being questioned concerning the truth therof they both said that the thing charged upon them was not true.

It is concluded by this Monthly Meeting that Thomas Scarbrough & Hellen his wife be admonished to frequent Freinds Meeting notwithstanding the blot that is upon them there being nothing possitively against them.

It is ordered that the next Monthly Meeting be at Thomas Wressle his house in Butterwick.

ATT a Monthly Meetting held att Butterwick the XII: day of the XII month 1672[1] :—

It is ordered that Thomas Wressle: & Richard Parnell goe from this Monthly Meeting to Michaell Monkton with a paper concerneing his owneing Peter Moody in his dissorderly marryage & also hard speeches given out by the said Michaell in opposition to Truth & bring his answer to the next Monthly Meeting.

It is ordered that Thomas Wresle & some Freinds of Epworth Meeting speak to Peter Moody & Robert Everatt concerning Peter his dissorderly marryage & bring in theyr answers the next Monthly Meeting.

It is ordered that contribution be maid throughout all the Meetings of Freinds belonging to the North west part of the County & brought in the next Monthly Meeting.

It is ordered that the next Monthly Meeting be att Richard Parnells: att Epworth.

p. 27

ATT a Meeting held att Epworth: the XII: day of the first month 1672/3[2] :—

Contributon brought in as followeth :—	£ s. d.
from Gainsburgh	01 : 00 : 03
Crowle:	00 : 16 : 04
Garthorpe	00 : 13 : 06
Brig	01 : 02 : 09
Epworth	00 : 10 : 00
Winteringham	00 : 15 : 00
	04 : 17 : 10

	£ s. d.
Disbursed to Crowle:	00 : 17 : 10

		s. d.
In the hands of William Garland		12 : 4
Sent up to the Quarterly Meeting	04 : 00 : 00	

[1] 12th February, 1673. [2] 12th March, 1673.

Michaell Monkton came to this Monthly Meeting & desired Meetings might still contynue att his house & att present Freinds assented to him.

Robert Everatt being spoken to about Peter Moody gave some satisfaction to Freinds of this Meeting.

It is ordered that next Monthly Meeting be held att Thomas Markehams house in Brigg :

ATT a Monthly Meeting held at Brigg the 9th day the 2th month 1673[1] :—

It is ordered that 3*s* be laid out by some Friend of the Metting of Wintringham towards the releife of a Friend belonging to their Metting till the next Monthly Meeting, it is alsoe ordered that some Friend belonging to Crowle Metting lie out 10*s* towards the supplie of two Friends that are in nessittie till the next Monthly Metting.

It is ordered that the next Monthly Meetting be at Thomas Wresles house in West Butterweeke.

p. 28

AT a Meeting held at West Butterwick the 14th day of the 3d moneth 1673[2] :—

It is ordered that Richard Parnell & Christopher Edwards goe to William Clark and admonish him to return to the Truth & bring in his answer to the next Monthly Meeting.

Thomas Wressell of Wintringham & Elizabeth Norton of the same came into the Meeting and declared there intentions of marriage and left it to the consideration of Freinds till the next Monethly Meeting.

William Potter of Gainsbr' came into the Meeting & brought a certificate under the hand of Mary Allen which joyntly acquainted Freinds with there intentions of marriage and left it to the consideration of Freinds untill the next Monthly Meeting.

Joseph Richardson, Glamford Briggs came into the Meeting & signified his intentions of marriage with Katherine Cooper of Monk Bretton & brought a certificate under the hands of Freinds belonging to the Monthly Meeting where they were both present signifying her willingness thereunto and hath left it to the consideration of the Monethly Meeting untill the next.

It is ordered that a generall contribution be made and brought up to the next Monethly Meeting.

It is ordered that the next Monethly Meeting be at the house of John Wressle in Thealby.

[1] 9th April, 1673. [2] 14th May, 1673.

p. 29

Att a Meeting held att John Wresles house at Thealby upon the 11th day of the fourth month: 1673[1] :—

		£	s.	d.
Contributons came in from	Gainsburgh	00	19	04
	Crowl & Epworth	01	02	02
	Garthorpe	00	13	06
	Winteringham	01	07	06
	Brigg	01	01	00
		05	03	06
Sent backe of this,	To Winteringham	00	14	00
	To Crowl:	00	10	00
	To Beltoft	00	05	00
	To Gainsburgh	00	09	06
	To Garthorpe	00	05	00
		02	03	06

£	s.	d.				
3	0	0	Sent to Lyncolne to the Quarterly Meeting	03	00	00

It is still concluded that Christopher Edwards & Richard Parnell doe goe as from this Monthly Meeting, to speak to William Clarke concerning that scandall which he hath brought upon Truth, that Truth may be cleare & Freinds alsoe bring in his answer the next Monthly Meeting.

Thomas Wresle of Wintringham & Elizabeth Norton came into the Meeting & a second tyme declared theyr intentons of marryage, there appearing noe objections: butt all things being cleare it was left to themselves with the advice of their owne Meeting to perfect the thing as may be seene meet;

William Potter of Gainsburgh and Mary Allen came a second tyme into the Meeting, & declared their intenton of marryage there appearing noe objections butt all things being cleare it was left to themselves with the advice of theyr owne Meeting to perfect the thing as might be seene meet.

Joseph Richardson came a second tyme into the Meeting, & without certficate declared his intention to take Katherine Coopr of Monk Bretton to wife, this Meeting had nothing before them of objection but believed he was cleare from others, soe it was left to themselves & Freinds to perfect the thing as may be seene meet the Meeting to which Katherine belongs haveing sent noe objection to the contrary:

It is ordered that the next Monthly Meeting be held att the house of Christopher Willson his house in Adlinfleet:

[1] 11th June, 1673.

p. 30

At a Meeting of Friends held at the house of Christopher Wilson of Adlingfleet the 9th day of the fifth month 1673[1] :—

William Clarke of Haxey came before Friends this day and humbly acknowledged his offence whereby he hath caused the enimyes of God to blaspheme, and hath set his hand to this following writing for the clearing of the Truth of God and his people, in the presence of the Lord & his people.

I William Clarke of Haxey who have formerly walked wth the people of God called Quakers ; whom I unfeignedly acknowledge are a people that fear the Lord being guided by that holy spirit of truth which only can lead into all Truth. But through the temptacons of the evill one & the deceits and corruptions of my owne heart I have beene misled from the way of that blessed Truth by that people owned & walked in ; and have contrary to the witness thereof in my owne conscience comitted lewdness with Margarett Browne to the great dishonor of God, the wounding of my owne conscience, and to the great scandall of his blessed Truth & people— And therefore I doe humbly acknowledge my transgression and my sinne unto the Lord against whom I have sinned, & before all this people whose mouths I have opened to speak against that holy Truth which I have formerly professed, & now by my ofence scandaliezed : I alsoe hereby testifie before all men, that the principall & way which the people called Quakers walk in is a principle of Truth, justice & holiness & standeth & for evr will stand a swift witness against all such impure actions, as I doe hereby confess my selfe guilty of & am heartily sorry for the same :

William Clarke : a Coppy : Exact & true by Willim Garland.

p. 31

The next Monthly Meeting ordered to be at the house of Henry Simpson in Gainsburgh.

Att a Monthly Meeting held att Gainsburgh the 14th day of the 6th month 1673[2] :—

	£	s.	d.
Given to Thomas Wresle of Winteringham disbursed by him to the necessity of Robert Oyle ..	00	03	00

It is desired that Freinds of Epworth Meeting bring in the account about Alice Barrows children the next Monthly Meeting.

It is ordered that contributions be maid throughout all the Meetings on the North west parts of the county of Lyncolne & brought in to the next Monthly Meeting.

[1] 9th July, 1673. [2] 14th August, 1673.

It is ordered the next Monthly Meeting be held att Richard Parnells house in Haxey.

It is desired that Freinds of Gainsburgh Meeting goe to John Barrow as from the Monthly Meeting & admonish, & exhort him to that which did att first convince him, that if possible he may retorne to Truth from whence he is gone :

p. 32

An account of what was done att a Monthly Meeting held att the house of Richard Parnell of Haxey the 10 : 7th : 1673[1] :—

Contributions Brought in the same tyme	£	s.	d.
Epworth & Crowle Meeting	01	00	10
Brigg Meeting	01	06	09
Garthorpe	00	11	05
Winteringam	00	18	00
Gainsburgh	00	18	06
	04	15	06
Retornd to Crowle	00	05	00
Returnd : to Gainsburgh	00	10	06
Ordered the Remainder be sent to Quarterly Meeting	04	00	00

It is ordered that Thomas Markham & Thomas Wresle doe againe vissitt John Barrow & advise & exhort & reprove him in all meekness & gentleness, to the intent he may be brought backe into the unity of the Truth & Freinds from whence he is gone & bring his fynall answer the next Monthly Meeting :

It is ordered that the next Monthly Meeting be att the house of[2]

It is ordered that next Monthly Meeting be att the house of Robert Ashton att Crowl[2] :

An account of what was done at a Monthly Meeting held at Robert Ashton his house in Crowle the 8th day of the 8th month 1673[3] :—

According to the order of the Monthly Thomas Wresle & Thomas Markham was at Gainsbrough to speak to John Barrow that he might turn to the Truthe but he absented himselfe that wee could not speak with him :

Orderd that some Freind belonging to Epworth Meeting lay down the sum of 10*s*. to a pore Freind for the releife of present necessity—

[1] 10th September, 1673. [2] *Sic.* [3] 8th October, 1673.

p. 33

Micajah Wake of Frodingham was at this Meeting and did then publish his intentions of marriage with Rebeckah Law of Pollington and have brough a certificate undr the hands of Freinds, of that Monethly Meeting where they were both present. And hath left it to the consideration of Freinds unto the next Monethly Meeting.

It is ordered that the next Monthly Meeting be at the house of Thomas Markham in Brigg.

ATT a Monthly Meeting of Freinds held att the house of Thomas Markham att Brigg the 13 day of 9ber 1673[1] :—

It is concluded that Epworth Meeting see to the sattisfying of John Browne & Alce Tates child deceased: as to charges for burying &c & give an account to the next Monthly Meeting that they may be imbursed:

It is ordered that generall Contributions be maid throughout all the Meetings of the North West part of this County & brought in to the next Monthly Meeting.

It is ordered that something be signified from this Monthly Meeting to Balby Meeting to search out the cause of John Law & his daughter dissent from the said daughters marryage with Micajah Wake according to former intentions & that Micajah give account to the next Meeting.

It is ordered that the next Monthly Meeting be held at Butterwick.

Contributions brought in from the severall Meetings as followeth :—

	£	s.	d.
Brigg Meeting	01	01	00
Crowle Meeting	00	18	05
Wintringham Meeting	01	00	00
Garthorp Meeting	00	13	02
Gainsbrough Meeting	00	18	02
	04	10	09
Paid to John Brown for his Charge about the deceased Child of Alice Tayte	00	15	00
Paid Wintringham Freinds for Robert Oyle	00	02	06
Paid to Crowle Meeting	00	05	00
Paid to Brigg Meeting	00	03	00
	01	05	6
remains —	03	05	03

[1] 13th November, 1673.

p. 34

An account of what was done at the Monthly Meeting at Butterwick the 10th of the 10th month 1673[1] :—

According to the order of the last Monthly Meeting Micajah Wake was at the Monthly Meeting at Balby, where Rebeckah Law was examined & her reasons tryed wherfore her mind was changed from marrying with Macajah Wake, and they were found soe weake & insufficient that she was judged of Freinds to have erred from the Truth & done manifest wrong to Micajah Wake & owned there judgement to be according to Truth.

It is ordered that the next Monthly Meeting be at the house of Thomas Markham in Brigg.

An account of what was done at a Monthly Meeting at Glamford Briggs the fourteenth day 11th month 1673[2] :—

Given unto Robert Ashton of Crowle five shillings for the reliefe of poor Friends there.

No further busines arising at this meeting Freinds departed having appointed the next meeting to be at West Boterwick at the house of Thomas Wresle.

An account of what was concluded att a Monthly Meeting held att Butterwick the 11 : day of the 12 : month 73[3] :—

Given into the hands of Christopher Edwards for the Releife of poore Freinds of Haxey Meeting & Crowle att that tyme 4*s.*

Richard Geeve of Housfleet came into the Meeting & brought a certificate from Freinds of North Cave Monthly Meeting signifying his intenons of marryage with Elizabeth Carlill of that Meeting & att present this Meeting had nothing against it but referrd him to the next Monthly Meeting.

John Cooper & Mary Drowly both of Fockerby came into the Meeting, & publyshed theyr intentions of marryage & it was taken into consideration untill the next Monthly Meeting.

Ordered a contribution be brought in to the next Monthly Meeting which is ordered to be att Thomas Scotts of Crowle ;

p. 35

Att a Monthly Meeting held att Crowle att the house of Thomas Scott the 11 : day of the first month 1673/4[4] :—

		£	s.	d.
Contributons then brought :	Gainsburgh	00	17	00
	Crowl	01	00	02
	Garthorpe	00	12	10
3 : 16 : 6	Wintringham ..	00	16	06
	Haxey	00	10	06

[1] 10th December, 1673. [2] 14th January, 1674. [3] 11th February, 1674. [4] 11th March, 1674.

	£ s. d.
Retornd backe to Garthorpe	00 : 02 : 06
Retornd to Wintringam	00 : 02 : 06
Retornd to Crowl :	00 : 05 : 00
	00 : 10 : 00

Given into the hands of William Garland to goe up to the Quarterly Meeting .. .. .. 03 : 06 : 00 & ordered that Brigg contributon be added.

Freinds of Epworth Meeting brought in an account concerneing Alce Tates children to the sattisfaction of Freinds in the Meeting.

Michuja Wake of Frodingam & Hannah Ruckhill of Adlinfleet came into the Meeting & acquainted Freinds with theyr intentions of marryage : who was desired to stay the answer of Freinds untill next Monthly Meeting.

John Cooper & Mary Drowly came a second tyme into the Meeting to acquaint Freinds with theyr intentions of Marryage & it appeareing to the Meeting they both ownd Truth & that all things were cleare, it was left to themselves & Freinds of that Meeting unto which they did belong to consumate the thing as they in the wysdome of God might see meet :

It was desired that Freinds of Garthorpe Meeting enquire whatts the reason that Richard Geeve proceeds nott in his intention of marryage with Elizabeth Carlill & bring an account next Monthly Meeting.

The next Monthly Meeting ordred to be att Brigg :

p. 36

An account of what was concluded at a Monthly Meeting held at Brigge the eighth day of the second month 1674[1] :—

Disbursed by Thomas Wresle of Boterwick (according to order of this Monthly Meeting) for the use of poor Friends of Crowle Meeting .. .. £ s. d. 00 : 05 : 00

Micajah Wake came the second time into the Meeting to acquaint Friends with the continuance of the purpose of marriage betwixt him & Hannah Ruckhill and all things appearing to be cleare, the consumation thereof was left to themselves and friends at their best conveniency.

The next Monthly Meeting appoynted to be at Gainsburgh at the house of H. Simpson.

[1] 8th April, 1674.

An account of what was concluded att a Monthly Meeting held att Gainsburgh the 12: day of the 3d month 1674[1] :—

It is concluded that Thomas Wresle may disburse 5*s*: for the use of poore Freinds of Crowl Meeting.

Edward Gillyatt & Isabell Oxley of Brigg came into the Meeting & declared theyr intentions of marryage & they was desired to wayt Freinds answer the next Monthly Meeting.

It is ordered that generall contributions be maid throughout all the Meetings of this Monthly Meeting & the remainder brought in to the next Monthly Meeting.

It is ordered that the next Monthly Meeting be held att Brigg:

Edmond Morly: books: 2*s*. : 4*d*½

John Wresle: 2*s*. : 4*d*½

John Ury: 2 : 4½

p. 37

Att a Monthly Meeting held att the house of Joseph Richardson in Brigg the 10: day of the 4th month 1674[2] :—

		£	s.	d.
Contributions came in then from	Brigg	01	02	00
	Winteringham ..	01	00	04
	Garthorpe ..	00	15	04
	Epworth & Crowl	01	03	06
	Gainsburgh ..	00	16	08
Paid in by William Garland of the Remaining Stocke		00	16	00
		5	13	10
Allowed Thomas Wresle which he disbursed ..		00	19	08
Given more to Thomas Wresle to Releive a poore man		00	04	00
Paid then into the hands of William Garland to goe up to the Quarterly Meeting 4*l*. 10*s*. 2*d*. ..		4	10	02

Richard Parnell of Axholme came into the Meeting & brought in a certificate from Balby Monthly Meeting that he had published his intentions of maryage with Mary Bettaly of Balby in that Meeting & the Meeting desired that he might wayt for answer the next Monthly Meeting.

Edward Gillyatt & Isabell Oxly of Brigg came a second tyme into the Meeting & published their intentions of marryage & nothing appearing to the Monthly Meeting, butt all things was cleare

[1] 12th May, 1674. [2] 10th June, 1674.

it was left to themselves & the advice of Freinds of their owne Meeting to accomplish the thing as may be found convenient.

Ordered that the next Monthly Meeting be held att Brigg.

p. 38

An account of what was concluded at a Monthly Meeting held at Brigge the 8th of the 5th month 1674[1] :—

It is desired by Friends at this Meeting assembled that Thomas Wresle of Boterwick disburse five shillings toward the supply of Symon Ross his necessityes and two shillings six pence for the relief of Jane Carnell, as in discretion he shall see it needfull, which is to be allowed him out of the next contribution.

It is ordered that Thomas Markham & William Smith of Elsham goe and visit Thomas Scarbrough and his wife the second time, and exhort and admonish them to return unto the unity of the Truth and fellowship of Friends with whom they have formerly walked and to give an account of their answer to the next Monthly Meeting.

Richard Parnell of Haxey came the second time into the Monthly Meeting signifying his purpose of marriage with Mary Bettaly and brought a certificate from Friends of Balby Meeting certifying the clearness of all things on her behalfe, now Friends of this Monthly Meeting finding all things cleare also on the part of Richard Parnell have left the consumation thereof to the discression of the parties & Friends at their best conveniency.

The next Monthly Meeting to be at Brigg and it is ordered that the settlement of all future Meetings at one constant place be debated and determined at the next Monthly Meeting.

p. 39

An account of what was concluded at a Monthly Meeting held at Brigge the twelth day of the 6th month 1674[2] :—

It is desired by Friends at this Meeting assembled that Thomas Wresle of Boterwicke disburse five shillings towards the supply of Symon Ross his necessityes which is to be allowed out of the next contribution.

It is desired that all Friends belonging to this Monthly Meeting doe bring in an account of the severall sufferings of Friends in their respective dwellings since the year 1672 unto the next Monthly Meeting; and so to be presented before the next Quarterly Meeting.

It is ordered that generall contributions be made throughout all the Meetings of this Monthly Meeting and such summes as

[1] 8th July, 1674. [2] 12th August, 1674.

have been disbursed by any particular Friend for the supply of the necessity of poor Friends, being deducted, the remainder to be brought to the next Quarterly Meeting.

Its ordered that the next Monthly Meeting be held att Glamford Briggs.

Att a Monthly Meeting held att Brigge the 9th Day of the 7th month 1674[1] :—

Contributions came in as followeth :	£	s.	d.
Winteringham	00	18	00
Garthorpe	00	15	04
Crowl & Epworth	00	18	06
Gainsburgh	00	17	10
Brigg	01	00	00
Paid in by William Garland in his hands	00	18	10
	05	08	06

Disbursed to Thomas Wresle & Edmond Morley 17*s.* 6*d.* Rests .. .. 04 : 11 : 00

Ordered the some of foure pounds eleven shillings to be sent up to the Quarterly Meeting.

It is ordered that the next Monthly Meeting be held att Butterwick att the house of Thomas Wresle :

Att a Monthly Meeting held at Butterwick the 14th day of the 8th month 1674[2] :—

It is ordered that Thomas Wresle of Butterwick disburse the sum of 5*s* for the supply of the pore belonging to there Meeting.

It is ordered that the next Monthly Meeting be at Thomas Markham house in Brigg.

p. 40

Att a Monthly Meeting held att Glamford Briggs the 11th day of the 9th month 1674[3] :—

It is desired by Friends of this Monthly Meeting that Henry Hudson disburse the summe of five shillings for the present supply of poore Friends of that meeting which is to be allowed out of the next contribution.

It is ordered that generall contributions be made in all the severall meetings belonging to this Monthly Meeting, and such sumes as have been disbursed by particular Freinds for supply of the poor being deducted the remainder to be brought into the next Quarterly Meeting.

[1] 9th September, 1674. [2] 14th October, 1674. [3] 11th November, 1674.

Ordered that the next Monthly Meeting be held at the house of Thomas Markham in Brigge.

p. 41

An account of what was concluded att a Monthly Meeting att the house of Thomas Markham of Brigg the 9: day of the tenth month 1674[1] :—

William Emly & Ruth Ridge late of Haxey came into the Meeting & did acquaint Freinds with their intentions of marryage & they was desired to awayt Freinds answer the next Monthly Meeting.

Contributons brought in as followeth :—	£	s.	d.
Winteringham	00	16	02
Garthorpe	00	14	00
Haxey	00	16	04
Gainsburgh	00	16	06
Brigg	01	00	00
old Stock	00	09	00
	04	12	00
Paid to Robert Everatt disbursed by Henry Hudson & Thomas Wresle	00	10	00
more for Belton poore	00	07	00
Left with Thomas Markham		05	00
	03	10	00

The remainder being £3 : 10 : 0 orderd to be carryed up to the Quarterly Meeting.

It is ordered that the next Monthly Meeting be held att the house of Thomas Wresle of Butterwicke.

An account of what was concluded at a Monthly Meeting held at Butterwick at the house of Thomas Wresle the 13th 11th month 1674/5[2] :—

It is ordred by Freinds of this Meeting that Robert Ashton lay down 5*s*. for the use of the poor of Crowle Meeting.

William Emley came to this Meeting the second time & brought with him a certificate under the hand of Ruth Ridge & severall other Freinds testifying that she doth retain her purpose to take the abovesaid William Emley to be her husband and desires to know the pleasure of the Monthly Meeting concerning them, who finding all things clear are willing they should accomplish the thing at their own convenience.

[1] 9th December, 1674. [2] 13th January, 1675.

p. 42

Robert Collier & Elizabeth Mitchill both of Glanford Briggs came to this Monthly Meeting & did signifie there intentions of marriage and left it to the consideration of Freinds untill the next Monthly Meeting.

It is concluded the next Monthly to be held at Thomas Markham house in Brigg.

At a Monthly Meeting held at the house of Thomas Markham at Glamford Briggs the 10th day of the 12th month 1674[1] it was then concluded :—

It is concluded & desired by Friends of this Meeting that Robert Ashton & Edward Chessman take care to procure a dwelling house for Symon Rosse & his familie in which service they are to be indempnifyed by Friends of this Monethly Meeting.

It is desired also that Robert Ashton & Friends of Crowle Meeting, take care for the supply of poore Friends of the Meeting, & give account thereof to this Monthly Meeting.

It is ordered that a generall contribution be collected throughout the severall Meetings, and brought unto to the next Monthly Meeting.

Robert Collyer and Elizabeth Mitchell came this day the 2d time into this Monthly Meeting signifying the continuance of their purpose of marriage which hath been considered by Friends, and all things being found cleare of both partyes, the consumation thereof is left to their own conveniency.

The next Monthly Meeting to be at Brigge.

p. 43

An account of what was concluded att a Monthly Meeting held att Thomas Markham the 10 day of the first month 1674/5.[2]

Itt is ordered that Edmond Morley, Thomas Wresle, Thomas Markham, Richard Parnell & William Garland take care to carry or send up an exact account of the sufferings of Freinds to the next Quarterly Meeting in order to the answering the desire of Freinds in London.

		£	s.	d.
Contributons brought in	Gainsburg :	01	05	06½
	Haxey :	01	06	01
	Winteringham	01	05	06
	Garthorpe	00	18	09
	Brigg	01	09	03
	Overplus	00	11	04
		06	16	05½

[1] 10th February, 1675. [2] 10th March, 1675.

	£	s.	d.
Disbursed to the necessity of William Birks ..	01 :	10 :	00
To Haxey & Crowle	00 :	16 :	06
To Garthorpe :	00 :	05 :	00
To Brigg :	00 :	03 :	00
	02 :	14 :	06

The Remainder £4 : 01 : 11½ orderd to be sent up to the Quarterly Meeting the 24 : Instant.

Thomas Thurgate of Hibaldstow came to this Meeting & acquainted Freinds wth his intentions of marriage with An Noble of Wellam in the County of Nottingham, & brought a certificate from the Monthly Meeting in that county that he had published the same his intentions together with the said An there : he was desired by this meeting to wayt Freinds answer the next Monthly Meeting :

John Ruckhill & Alce Coosens came into the Meeting and declared their intentions of marryage the Meeting desired they might appeare once together att the Marsh Monthly Meeting & bring there a certificate that all things are cleare on the woemans part & alsoe wayt the answer of the next Monthly Meeting.

It is ordered that the next Monthly Meeting be held att the house of Richard Parnell att Haxey.

p. 44

An accompt of what was concluded at a Meeting holdne at Axholme this 14th 2th month 1675[1] :—

It is ordered by us that Edward Chessman doth lay down to Symon Ross the some of 5*s* & 3*s* that he hath laid down before.

John Ruchill hath apparred the second time before us with a certificate from Mumby Monthly Meeting holdne at Partnay Mills at Thomas Brown house and finding that all things of both sids is cleare we have given our assents for them to take one another at time and place convainient.

Thomas Peper & Frances Parrot both of this Monthly Meeting came before us and signified their intentions of marriage soe desired time till the next Monthly Meeting to give in our answer.

It is ordered by this Meeting that the next Monthly Meeting be at John Wresle house in Thealby.

[1] 14th April, 1675.

An account of what was concluded at the Monthly held at Thealby at the house of John Wresle the 12 3d month 1675[1] :—

The busines of Thomas Thurgate his marriage (being accomplished without a certificate from the Monthly Meeting) be contrary to that wholesome order of Truth amonst Freinds, was had into consideration & judged and the abovesaid Thomas hath acknowledged his weakness in soe doing undr his hand

Thomas Thurgate

It is ordered that Robert Ashton lay down 5*s.* for the present supply of the pore belonging to Crowle Meeting.

It is ordered that a contribution be collected & brought into the next Monthly Meeting.

It is ordered that the next Monthly Meeting be held at Edmond Morley house in Adlinfleet.

Thomas Pepper & Francis Parrot came the 2d time into the Monthly Meeting & published there intentions of marriage & all things being found cleare, it was left to themselves to consider with Freinds of their Meeting to consumate it at time convenient.

p. 45

An account of whatt was concluded att a Monthly Meeting held att the house of Edmond Morly att Adlingfleet the 09 : day of the 4 month 1675[2] :—

Contributions brought in as followeth :

	£	s.	d.
Garthorpe :	00	15	02
Winteringham	00	19	10
Brigg	00	18	06
Gainsburgh	00	18	00
Crowle	01	00	08
Paid in by William Garland remaind in his hands..	00	13	00
	05	05	02

Paid back to Robert Ashton for the poore of that Meeting 5*s.* : 13*s.* :

Paid backe to Garthorpe Meeting 7*s.* 2*d.* for the poore of that meeting.

Ordered that the som of foure pounds being the remainder be sent up to the Quarterly Meeting.

It is ordered that the next Monthly Meeting be held att Gainsburgh att the house of Henry Sympson :

[1] 12th May, 1675. [2] 9th June, 1675.

Att a Monthly Meeting held att the house of Henry Sympson of Gainsburgh the 14: day of the fift month 1675[1] :—

It is concluded that 3s. be sent from this Monthly Meeting to Wintringham to supply the necessity of their poore & 5s. to Crowl for the same service.

William Garland of Gainsbrough came into the Monthly Meeting & acquainted Freinds that he proposed to take Mary Damson[2] of Richmond to wife & brought a certificate from the Monthly Meeting to which the said Mary belongs testifying that the said William together with the said Mary in that Monthly Meeting had alsoe testified the same to which this Monthly Meeting declared they had Unity with it only desired tyme until the next Monthly Meeting to give answer.

John Wresle of Winteringham Meeting came into the Monthly Meeting & acquainted Freinds with his intentions to take Susanna Cousen to wife it is expected that the said John doe bring a certificate from that Monthly whereto the said Susan doth belong that all things are cleare & to receive an answer the next Monthly Meeting. (*In the margin:* Barnaby in the Beck.)

It is ordered that the next Monthly Meeting be held att the house of Mary Parnell of Haxey:

p. 46

Att a Monthly Meeting att the house of Mary Parnell held the 11: day of the 6: month 1675[3] :—

It is ordered that generall contributions be maid throughout the severall Meetings & brought up to the next Monthly Meeting:

William Garland came to our Monthly Meetting this day the 11 day of the 6 mo 75[2]2 tim in to the monthly Meeting signifying the continuance of his purpose of his marrye with Mary Damson[2] which haith beene considered by Friends and all things being found cleare of both partys the consumation theireof is left to their owne conveniency.

John Wresle of Thealby came a second tyme into the Monthly Meeting & published his intentions to take Susanna Cossens of Barneby by the Becke to wife & also brought a certificate from the Monthly Meeting to which shee belongs, which upon consideration it was found that all things was cleare on both parts & the consumating thereof was left to himselfe with the advice of Freinds as they should see convenient:

It is ordered that the next Monthly Meeting be held att the house of Thomas Wresle of Butterwicke:

[1] 14th July, 1675. [2] *recte* Adamson. [3] 11th August, 1675.

Thomas Cooper of Aukborough acquainted this Meeting thee first tyme that he intended to take Sarah Store of Knottingley to wife & brought a certificate from the Monthly Meeting to which shee belongs that together with the said Sarah he had published the same intentions in that Monthly Meeting this Meeting hath taken tyme to consider of the thing untill the next Monthly Meeting.

p. 47

At a Monthly Meeting held att Butterwicke the 8 day of the 7th month 1675 [1]:—

		£	s.	d.
Contributions as followeth :	Wintringham..	01	00	04
	Garthorpe	00	14	00
	Crowl	01	05	10
	Gainsburgh	00	16	08
	Brigg	01	00	00
		4	16	10

Disbursed to supply necessity: 26*s.* 10*d.* Reste sent up to the Quarterly Meeting the same in Thomas Wresle hands 13*s.* 2*d.* .. .. 3 : 10 : 00

It is ordered that Freinds of each particular Meeting take care to signify att their respective meeting of the desire that is amongst Freinds to order a woemans Meeting on the West side the County of Lyncolne & acquaint the Quarterly Meeting of their proceedings therein.

Thomas Cooper of Aukburgh came a second tyme to our Monthly Meeting & signifyed his intention to take Sarah Story of Knottingley to wife & alsoe brought a certificate that he had a second tyme published the same thing at Knottingley Monthly Meeting, & upon enquiry maid, this Meeting was sattisfied that things was cleare on his part, soe was left to the consumation of the matter as himselfe & Freinds might see convenient:

It is ordered that thee next Monthly Meeting be held at the house of Robert Ashton of Ealand.

At a Monthly Meeting held at Robert Ashton house in Ealand the 13th day of the 8th month 1675[2] :—

It is ordered that Robert Ashton & Thomas Wresle of Butterwick make saile of the goods of Alice Hallewell lately deceased for the use of the children and to agree with James Dixon for keeping the youngest boy for one year.

[1] 8th September, 1675. [2] 13th October, 1675.

It is ordered that the next Monthly Meeting be held at the house of Thomas Markham in Brigg and that weomen Freinds come up to the said Meeting in order to the setling of a weomens Monthly Meeting.

---

p. 48

London the 27th: 7th Month 1675.[1]

At a solemn generall meeteing of many faithfull freinds & brethren concerned in the publique labour of the gospell & service of church of Christ for the most part of this nation.

Beloved Freinds & Brethren

Upon weighty consideration had of the affairs relating to the Church of Christ in our day in the counsell wisdome & ordring of Gods holy Spirit whose grolious[2] bright & refreshing presence was plentifully manifest among us: we doe with one consent agree to & conclude upon these following perticulars, seriously recommending them to the care & diligence of all freinds & brethren in the Truth in thier respective places & services whether in these or other parts of the world where this may come hopeing that upon reading hereof they will have some sence of that heavenly power presence & wisdome of God that filled our hearts & gave us heavenly unity both in receiveing & giveing forth this our advice & counsell & that through the sensible fellowshipp in the same power & wisdome of God in themselves they may be stirred up to put the same in practice in thier severall places to exalting of that blessed name in which wee have found salvation & to the debasing & bringing under whatever hath lifted up it selfe against that most holy name & led from the unity of the faith & good order that stands therein.

Forasmuch as we are deepely sensible of the sorrows & sufferings that have comed upon the Church of Christ in severall places by reason of certain disorderly proceedings of some professing the Truth which have occationed many questions & Debates among some Freinds & our advise being desired thereupon wee doe in the name & councell of God hereby signify our sence advice & judgement as follows:

1st Concerning Marriages of Kindred

It is our liveing sence & judgement in the truth of God that not only the marriages of neare kindred expressly forbiddin under the Law ought not to be practised under the Gospell but that in as much as any marriges of neare kindred in the time of the Law (*p. 49*) was in condescention & upon extraordinary occasions as

[1] 27th September, 1675. [2] *sic recte* glorious.

upholding their tribes & that the nearer their marriages were the more unholy they were accounted, wee in our day ought not to approach our neare kindred in any such respect particularly first cozens, being redeemed out of those kindreds tribes & earthly lots for the upholding of which marriages within the Kindred were once dispenced with & brought to the spirituall dispensation which gives dominion over the affections & leads to these marriages which are more naturall & are of better report & though some through weakness have beene drawne into such marriages which being done must not be broken yet let not their practice be any precedent or example to any other amongst us for the time to come.

2 Concerning contracts in order to marriage

That such Freinds as have with serious advice and deliberation free & mutuall consent as in the sight of God & unity of his blessed Truth, absolutly agreed espoused or contracted upon the account of marriage shall not be allowed or owned among us in any unfaithfullness or unjustice one to another to break or violate any such contract or engagement which is to the reproach of Truth or injury of one another & where ane such breach or violation of such solemn contract is knowne or complained of or enmity or strife occationed thereby wee advise & counsell that a few faithfull Freinds both men & woemen in their respective Meeteings to which the parties belong be appointed to enquire into the cause thereof & in the wisdome & councell of God to put a stop & speedy end thereto & bring Gods power & the judgment thereof over them that have offended in this case untill they come to unfeigned repentance, and further wee advise & exort that no engagements made without honest endeavours to obtaine or due regard first had to the councells & consent of parents relations & Friends be countenanced that soe all foolish and unbridled affections & all ensnareing & selfish ends be not so much as found among you on any hand.

3 Concerning Mens & Woemens Meetings

It is the judgement & testimony in the word of Gods wisdome of the rise & practice seting up & establishing of mens & woemens Meeteings in the Church of Christ in this our generation is according to the mind & counsell of God & done in the ordring & leading of his eternal Spirit & that is the duty of all Friends & brethren in the powr of God in all parts to be dilligent therein & to encourage & further each other in that blessed worke, & particularly that Friends & brethren in their respective counties encourage their faithfull & grave woemen in the settlement of the said Meeteings & if any professing the Truth shall *(p. 50)* either by word or deed directly discountenance, or weaken the hands of either men or woemen, in that work & service of the Lord let such be admonished according to the order of the gospell & if they receive it not but refuse councell & persist in that work of division we cannot but looke upon them as therein not in unity with the Church of Christ & order of the Gospell & therefore let Freinds goe on in the power of God & in that work for him his Truth & people & not be staid or hindred by them or their opposition.

4 Concerning Sighing groaning & Singing in the Church

It hath beene & is our liveing sence & constant testimony according to our experience of the divers operations of the Spirit & power of God in his Church that there hath beene & is serious sighing sensible groaning & reverent singing breathing forth an heavenly sound of joy with grace with the Spirit & with the understanding in blessed unity with the brethren while they are in the publick labour & service of the Gospell whether by preaching praying or praysing God in the same power & spirit & all to edification & comfort in the Church of Christ which therefore is not to be quencht or discouraged by any, but where any doe or shall abuse the Power of God or are imoderate or doe either in imitation which rather burthens than edifys such ought to be privately admonisht unless rebellious for that life power & spirit is risen in the Church which doth distinguish & hath power accordingly to judge.

5 Concerning our Testimony against Tithes

That our ancient testimony against tythes which we have borne from the begining & for which many have deeply suffred not only spoiling of their goods but imprisonment even unto death be carefully & punttually upheld & if all that those that oppose sleight or neglect that antient testimony be lookt upon & dealt withall as unfaithfull to the antient & universal testimony of Truth according to Gospell order extablisht amongst us.

11 Concerning Tradeing

That freinds & brethren in theire respective Meetings watch over one another in the love of God & care of the gospell particularly that none trade beyond their ability nor stretch beyond their compass & that they use few words in dealings & keepe their word in all things least they bring through their forwardness dishoner to the precious Truth of God.

p. 51

6 Concerning our Testimony or Publick Meeteing in time of Suffering

That as it hath beene our care & practice from the beginning that an open Testimony for the Lord should be borne & a publick standard for Truth & righteousness upheld in the word & Spirit of God by our open & knowne Meetings against the Spirit of persecution that in all ages hath sought to lay wast Gods heritage & that only through faithfullness constancy & patience victory hath beene & is obtained soe it is our advice & judgment that all friends gathered in the name of Jesus keepe up those publicke Testimonys in their respective places & not decline forsake or remove their publick assemblies because of times of suffring as wordly fearfull politick professors have done because of informers & the like persecutors for such practices are not consistent with the nobillity of the Truth & therefore not to be owned in the Church of Christ.

7 Concerning Recording the Churches Testimonies & the Parties Condemnation

That the Churches Testimonys & Judgment against disorderly and scandalous walkers as also the repentance & condemnation of the parties restored be recorded in a distinct booke in the respective Monthly or Quarterly Meetings for the clearing of Truth Friends & our holy profession to be produced or published by Friends for that end & purpose soe farr only as in Gods heavenly wisdome they shall see needfull & its alsoe our advice in the love of God that after any Friends repentance & restoration (he abideing faithfull) in the Truth that condemns the evill, none amongst you soe remember his transgression as to cast it at him or upbraid him with it for thats not according to the mercys of God.

8 Our Judgment against Contemptible names given against our Heavenly Ordr care & Instructions in the matr

It is our sence admonition & Judgment in the fear of God & the authority of his powr & spirit to Friends & Brethren in their several meetings that noe such slight & contemptible & expressions as calling mens & woemens Meetings Corts Sessions or Synods, that they are popish impositions useless & burdensome that faithfull Friends (which we testify have beene given forth from the Spirit & powr of God are mens edict & cannons or embraceing them bowing to men elders in the service of the Church Popes or Bishops with such scorn full saivings be permitted among them but that Gods powr be set upon the top of that unsavoury spirit.

p. 52

9 Concerning Propounding Marriages

It is our Judgment that for better Satisfaction to all parties & that there may be due time for enquiry of clearness of the persons concerned it is convenient that marriages be at least 2s propounded to the Meeteings that are to take care therein (both to the mens & woemens Meeteings where both are establisht) & when things are cleared that the marriage be accomplished in a grave & publick assemblies of Friends & relations.

10 Concerning Disputes

That Friends as far as in them lies in their several places take greate care not to entangle themselves or others in debates or disputes with froward contentious Spirits being men of corrupt mindes destitute of the Truth whethr professors or othrs that the Church be not disturbed by unprofitable controversies but that Friends stand over that crooked envious Spirit in the dominion of Gods powr & peacable Truth & place judgment in that upon theire heads yet where controversies cant with clearness & honr to the Truth be avoided that Friends stand in Gods wisdome & powr the defence of the Truth and those freinds & brethren that are engaged in the defence of the Lords Truth & their labors be not discouraged.

12 Of Friends Antient Testimony against the Corrupt Fashions & Language of the World

And lastly it is much upon us to put Friends in remembrance to keepe the antient testimony Truth begott in our hearts in the beginning against the Spirit of this world & for which many many have suffred cruell mockings beatings & stoneings & particularly as to the currupt fashions dealings & language of the world Their reachings & vaine jestings that the Cross of Christ in all things may be kept to which preserves Friends blameless & honrs the Lords name & Truth in the earth. These are an abstract of those things that were propounded & much more largely & livelingly spoken to and agreed upon wth great tenderness clearness & unity in the love Spirit powr & Wisdom of God at the aforesaid Meeteing all which wee recomend to the evidence of Gods holy witness in the hearts of his people resting. . . . . .

p. 53

Your faithfull brethren in the love & labour of the Gospell & freinds present at the said Meeteing.

A. Parker	J. Claypoole	T. Langhorn	P. Belt
T. Salthouse	W. Gosnell	J. Bankes	J. Longhurst
S. Crisp	L. Howard	J. Jennix	G. Whatherly
G. Whitehead	T. Everden	W. Gajes	W. Yardley
J. Burnyat	T. Atkins	T. Gilpin	F. Finchen
W. Penn	J. Pickton	J. Kilborn	S. Wallenfeild
J. Lancaster	G. Nicholson	J. Elson	I. Penington
G. Roberts	E. Bourne	M. Weeve	J. Rabet
A. Rigge	J. Furley Jnr.	W. Gibson	J. Wilsford
R. Wether	J. Merricke	W. Stone	J. Penford
H. Stout	G. Barnadiston	G. Burr	R. Longworth
T. Rudyard	J. Fletcher	J. Batt	O. Sanseim
J. Parke	S. Thronton	C. Baron	T. Hemp

C. Taylor	T. Robinson	G. Embory	N. Buxon
R. Thomas	J. Loft	C. Dakins	I. Harrison
J. Moone	T. Holl	J. Garret	T. Briggs
A. Lawrence	W. Gandy	W. Bunting	J. Smith
B. Bayley	J. Graves	J. Symchoce	J. Boldrum
S. Smith	J. Greenen	F. Bracy	J. Mordink
W. Fallowfeild	W. Watson		E. Hooks
J. Hale			

Postscript

There is yet a weight & necessity laid upon us from the Lord God in the bowells of Jesus Christ to beseech & warne all freinds who are or may be concerned in these weighty matters from the aforesaid meeteing & about the affaires of the Church that you al walk unblameable in these things & be examples & encouragements of heavenly & Gospel ordr to the flock of God that authority in the Truth & into rest with his witness in mens consciences for their convincement may be preserved in the name & powr of our Lord Jesus Christ & therein eye & seek the salvation & eternall good of Souls which he that winneth is wise & none of you to manage things in strife or vaine glory or in a zeal without true knowledge or gospel ordr as to the manner of your proceedings as well as the matter intended that noe reale accation of advantage may be given to such as have offended faln short or beene weake in any thing for its knowne to the Lord our God that wee have a care upon our hearts & travell in our souls that our testimony for him in thes matrs may not be enjured lesened or made ivalid through imprudence on any hand as to the managemet thereof our care being for souls & haveing a generall eye unto Truth & the Churches peace in these things before mentiond wherefore let the peaceable wisdome that comes from above and is gently & easy to be entreated be eyed: followed *(p. 54)* and justified by you and amongst you all & not that which is from beneath & in the divine light power & spirit which hath judgment mercy & forgiveness in it so ministr in their season you will feele our life & have unity with us & a sence of & care for the Churches peace & prosperity & the salvation of soules which is of great value.

Blessed are the Peace makers for they shall be called the Children of God.

A. Parker
G. Whitehead
T. Salthouse
J. Batt
W. Penn
J. Parke
W. Gibson

p. 55

ATT a Monthly Meeting held att the house of Thomas Markham in Brigg the 10: day of the ninth month 1675[1]:—

Itt is concluded that in respect to the shortness of the dayes in the winter season, the grave woemen of each particular Meeting, in their owne respective meetings, assemble together, to consider wherein they may serve the Truth & whatt they have to comunicate to the Mens Meeting may by them be sent up to the Monthly Meeting the day to assemble in may be left to their owne discretion.

Anthony Turner & Ann Pooll both of Martin came into the Meeting & acquainted Friends with their intentions of marriage & the thing was left to be enquired into whether all things was cleare, & they desired to wayt Freinds answer the next Monthly Meeting:

It is ordered that the next Monthly Meeting be held att Butterwicke.

It is ordered that generall contributions be made throughout every particular Meeting & brought up to the next Monthly Meeting:

ATT a Monthly Meeting held at Thomas Wresle house in West Butterwick the 8th day of 10ber 1675[2]:—

Contributions as Followeth:

	£	s.	d.
Gainsburgh Meeting	00	17	10
Brigg Meeting ..	01	00	10
Crowle Meeting ..	00	17	00
Wintringham: ..	00	17	06
Garthorp Meeting ..	00	13	05
	04	06	07
Given to Freinds of Epworth Meeting for the supplying of necessityes with them	00	17	00
Given to Freinds of Wintringham Meeting &c. ..	00	05	00
Given to Freinds of Garthorp Meeting &c. ..	00	05	00
Given to Freinds of Brigg Meeting	00	07	06
disburst..	01	14	06
Remains to be sent to the Quarterly Meeting ..	02	12	01

p. 56

IT is concluded that the mare which was borrowed by John Robinson of Epworth to carry him up to London upon Truths account and made unserviceable be paid for out of a publicke

[1] 10th November, 1675. [2] 8th December, 1675.

stock and the way how the moneys must be raised left to the consideration of the next Monthly Meeting.

Anthony Turner of Martin came into the Monthly Meeting the 2d time and signified his intentions of marriage with Ann Poole of the same and all things being found clear, the consumation of the marriage is left to themselves & to Freinds of that meeting.

It is ordered that the next Monthly Meeting be held at Thomas Markham house in Brigg.

At a Monethly Meeting of Friends held at the house of Thomas Markham at Glamford Briggs the 12th day of the 11th month 1675[1] :—

It is concluded that a contribution be made for the suffering Friends at Northhampton and brought in to the next Monethly Meeting.

William Kelsey of Epworth & Helene Cuttford of the same came this day before Friends and signified their intentions of marriage the first time, and submitted their said purpose to the consideration of Friends untill the next Monethly Meeting.

It is concluded & desired that some Friends of each perticular meeting doe make enquiry of all such sums of mony as have been given or bequeathed by any deceased Friends or others for the service of the Truth and that an account thereof be brought in to the next Monethly Meeting.

It is ordered that the next Monthly Meeting be held at the house of Thomas Markham at Brigge.

p. 57

At a Monthly Meeting held at the house of Thomas Markhams of Brigg the 9th of 12th month 1675[2] :—

An account of what moneys came in for Northampton Freinds

	£	s.	d.
Gainsbrough Meett ..	01	02	00
Brigg meetting.. ..	01	10	00
Butterwick Meetting ..	00	18	03
Adlinfleet Meetting	01	00	00
Winteringham Metting	01	00	00
in all	05	10	03

It is ordered that Thomas Wresle of Butterwick lye down 10*s.* for the poor of there Meetting.

[1] 12th January, 1676. [2] 9th February, 1676.

William Kelsey of Epworth came into the Monthly the second time & signified his intentions of marriage with Hellen Cutforth of the same, & all things being found clear, the consumation of the marriage is left to themselves & to Freinds of that Meetting.

It is ordered that a contribution be brought in for the supply of Freinds to the next Monthly Meeting.

It is concluded that the next Monthly Meetting be held at the house of Thomas Wresle of Butterwick.

p. 58.

An account of whatt was concluded att a Monthly Meeting held att the house of Thomas Wresle of Butterwick on the 8 day of the first month 1675/6[1] :—

Contributions came in as followeth

		£	s.	d.
	Gainsburgh	00	15	08
1 : 6 : 0	Crowl :	00	17	02
15 : 8	Garthorpe	00	14	00
	Winteringam	00	19	02
2 : 1 : 8	Brigg	01	00	00
		04	06	00

Retorned baccke to Crowl & Winteringam : 26*s.* : Rest 03 : 00 : 00

It is ordered that Thomas Wresle deposit 11*s.* 6*d.* to John Robinson that he is out of purse for the cure of a mare some Meetings since mention :

It is desired that the severall woemen belonging to the particular Meetings on the North west parts of the County of Lyncolne doe together with men Freinds assemble together att the next Monthly Meeting.

It is ordered that the next Monthly Meeting be held att Brigg.

Att a Meeting held att the house of Thomas Markeham att Brigg the 12 day of the second month 1676[2] :—

It is desired that Freinds of every particular Meeting take care to relieve their owne poore & that this meeting may imburse them next contribution.

It is ordered that for the present were Freinds doe meet together once a month before the mens Monthly Meeting that if any busineses of which doe fall out of that it may by them be brought to the mens Meeting :

[1] 8th March, 1676. [2] 12th April, 1676.

It is ordered that the next Monthly Meeting be held att the house of Henry Sympson of Gainsburgh.

p. 59.

Att a Meeting held att the House of Henry Sympson of Gainsburgh the 10 of the 3d month 1676[1] :—

It is ordered that there be contribution maid through out all the particular meetings of the Monthly Meeting & brought up to the next Monthly Meeting.

It is ordered that the next Monthly Meeting be held att the house of William Spaine att Garthorpe.

Att a Meeting held att Garthorpe the 14 : day of the 4th month 1676[2] this is that disorderly Meeting which was held at William Spaines house[3] :—

Contributions came in as followeth

		£	s.	d.
	Garthorpe ..	00	14	06
	Winteringham	00	18	10
	Gainsburgh ..	00	14	08
	Crowle ..	01	01	10
2 : 5 : 10	Brigg ..	01	00	00

Retorned baccke to Winteringham 5*s.*
Garthorpe 2 : 6
Crowle 17 : –

It is ordered that William Garland receive the Brigg contribution & add it to the above contribution & carry up to the Quarterly Meeting.

It is ordered that William Spaine appeare att the next Monthly & that then the matter wherein Freinds are dissatisfied concerneing him be heard & in the meanetyme all Freinds concerned may have notice to come alsoe to the Monthly Meeting to the intent that truth may be cleared & Freinds preserved in Unity therein :

It is ordered that the next Monthly Meeting be held att the house of Robert Ashton of Ealand.

p. 60.

Att a Monthly Meeting held att the house of Robert Ashton of Ealand the 12. 5 month 1676[4] :—

Whereas there was lately a Monthly Meeting appointed att the house of William Spaine by the Monthly Meeting last held att Gainsburgh for want of through information concerneing

[1] 10th May, 1676. [2] 14th June, 1676.
[3] *Sic:* see the minute of the next meeting.
[4] 12th July, 1676.

him who it appeares had not given that sattisfaction he ought to have done to Freinds in a certaine matter brought against him, nor was in present unity with Freinds: It is therefore ordered for the tyme to come that every particular Meeting be very cautious who they are that comes to Monthly Meetings to serve the Truth that they be such as are willing & capable to serve the Truth men of good lives & conversacions & in present unity with Freinds that Truth may also be kept cleare & Freinds preserved in unity therein.

2: Whereas William Spaine was ordered to appeare att this Monthly Meeting in order to giveing Freinds that sattisfaction he ought to have done in a matter brought against him, which was very scandalous, & formerly & alsoe att the Meeting desired to deal ingeniously & confess if he were guilty & to sett Truth over wickednesse, & whereas instead of comeing to the Meeting he only sent an excusing lettr. nott att all cleareing Truth butt in the roome thereof condemning Freinds who seeke the honor. of Truth alone, it is therefore the Judgment of this Meeting that the said paper or lettr. sent to the Meeting is wholly to be condemnd: & this Meeting doth condemne it, & untill William Spaine have given sattisfaction about Matter charged against him, to the Monthly Meeting this Meeting alsoe declares him such a one & with whom they cant: att present have present Unity, its alsoe judged that Edmond Morley & Robert Reeder acquaint William Spaine with the judgement of the Meeting accordingley.

It is ordered that the next Monthly Meeting be held att the House of George Nicholson of Burton Stather.

p. 61.

At a Monthly Meeting held at the house of George Nicholson of Burton Stather the 9th of 6th month 76[1]:—

It is ordered that a contribution be brought in for the supply of Freinds to the next Monthly Meetting.

Whereas some Freinds of Epworth Meetting have not freedome to meet at the house of Mary Parnel because of her accompanying with one Hezekiah Browne whereby the Truth is very much scandalisd this Meetting therefore hath ordered that Thomas Wresle & Henry Hudson goe to the said Mary Parnel & bring in her answer to the next Monthly Meetting.

William Spaine came to this Meetting, and as to the matter charged against him, he sollemly and seariously as in the presence of the lord & before us declared himself to be clear both in thought and deed, saveing some light words which he spoke to her (upon which she might ground the slander) for which he

[1] 9th August, 1676.

acknowledgeth himself to blame alsoe he condems himself for his reflecting upon Freinds by his letter to the last Monthly Meeting & is sorry for any thing that he hath offended Freinds in, & desires Unity with them which gave the whole Meeting full satisfaction ;

It is ordered that the next Monthly Meeting be held at the house of Thomas Wresles of Butterwick & that weomen Freinds come up to that Meetting.

p. 62.

Att a Monthly Meeting held att the house of Thomas Wresle of Butterwick 13 day 7 month 1676[1] :—

Contributions came in as followeth

	£	s.	d.
Epworth ..	00 :	16 :	09
Garthorpe ..	00 :	13 :	..
Winteringham	00 :	18 :	10
Gainsburgh ..	00 :	15 :	06
Brigg ..	01 :	01 :	..
	4 :	05 :	01

Retornd to Epworth 17*s.* 6*d.* Garthorp 2*s.* 6*d.* more to Epworth 5*s.* 1*d.* Resting for the Quarterly Meeting .. .. 03 : 00 : 00

Whereas Thomas Wresle & Henry Hudson was ordered to speake to Mary Parnell concerning her intended marryage with Hezekia Browne her answer was she was resolved to marry with the said Hezekia & it appeareing that the man is nott soe much as a professor of Truth this Meeting concludeth that the said intended marryage is contrary to Truth & Freinds cant butt condemn it.

It is ordered that the next Monthly Meeting be held att the house of Christopher Edwards of Epworth.

Att a Monthly Meeting att the house of Christopher Edwards in Epworth the 11th of 8tr br 1676[2] :—

It is ordered that the next Monthly Meeteing be held att the house of Thomas Markham in Brigg.

At a Monthly Meeting held at the house of Thomas Markham in Brigg the 8th 9th month 1676[3] :—

It is ordered that Thomas Bainton goe to John Dent of Thealby and let him know it is the desire of this Monthly Meeting

[1] 13th September, 1676. [2] 11th October, 1676. [3] 8th November, 1676.

that he would come up to the next Monthly Meeting to satisfy Freinds concerning his demeanour towards Freinds & Truth at the last Assizes.

It is ordered that Robert Ashton and Thomas Wresle goe to Macajah Wake and admonish him to be more frequent in comeing to Freinds Weekly Meetings.

It is ordered that Joseph Richardson and Thomas Markham speak to Nicholas Jackson that he come to the Monthly Meeting and then give Freinds satisfaction as to his disorderly conversation amongst Freinds.

p. 63.

It is ordered that Thomas Scurbrough & Ellinor his wife be desired to come to the next Monthly Meeting and show reasons if they can why they walk disorderly, & doe not come to Freinds Meetings & Thomas Markham & William Smith are desired to speak to them accordingly.

It is ordered that Robert Ashton disburs five shillings towards the relief of the poor of Crowle Meeting untill the next Contribution.

It is ordered that a contribution for the releif of pore Freinds be collected & brought up to the next Monthly Meeting.

It is ordered that the next Monthly Meeting be held at the house of Thomas Markham in Brigg.

At a Monthly Meeting of Freinds held at the house of Thomas Markham of Glamford Briggs the 13th day of the 10th month 1676[1]:—

Contributions brought in as followeth :

	£	s.	d.
Gainsburgh meeting ..	00	10	02
Adlingfleet	00	13	05
Wintringham	00	14	04
Brigg Meeting ..	00	15	06

Disbursed out of this Contribution for the present relief of the poor in Brigg Meeting .. .. 00 : 05 : 00

also for the reliefe of the poore in Adlinfleet Meeting .. .. 00 : 02 : 06

John Dent appeared at this Monthly Meeting, according to former desire of Freinds, and as to Friends dissatisfaction with his demeanor the last Assizes at Lincolne, his answer is (as before the Lord) that he did not either directly or indirectly know of his fathers dealings with the Bailiffs in order to the procurement of his liberty, nor consent unto it when he did know.

Nicholas Jackson did not this day come to the Meeting according to Freinds desire, but refused to come & further told Vincent

[1] 13th December, 1676.

Brownlow that he was resolved to marry the woeman, and to come at Freinds Meetings no more, notwithstanding Friends see it necessary that some honest Friends once again visit him and admonish him to return to the unity of Friends in Gods everlasting Truth & bring his answer to the next Monthly Meeting.

For as much as there hath been some neglect of Friends in speaking to Thomas Scurburgh & his wife according to former desire. It is againe desired that Thomas Markham & William Smith visit them both and admonish them in all tenderness to return to the unity of Friends in the eternall Truth of God which they have formerly professed, & bring there answer to the next Monthly Meeting.

p. 64.

Wheras there is a difference depending betwixt John Johnson & John Dent which doth tend to breach of unity betwixt them therfore it is desired that they both appear at the next Monthly Meeting in order to a friendly agreement that they may for time to come walk together in the unity of the Truth.

Thomas Thurowgate of Hibaldstow in the County of Lincoln came this day to the Monthly Meeting and acquainted them with his purpose of marriage with Hannah Potter of Lea in the same county, which Friends have taken into consideration till the next Monthly Meeting, where the said Hannah is desired to be present.

The next Monthly Meeting to be at the house of Thomas Markham in Brigge.

Att a Monthly Meeting of Friends held at the house of Thomas Markham of Glamford Briggs the tenth day of the 11th month 1676[1] :—

William Potter is desired to acquaint Thomas Taylor of Gainsburgh that Friends of the Monthly Meeting have a great desire to speak with him, and in order thereto they doe unanimously desire him to meet them at the next Monthly Meeting.

This Monthly Meeting having severall tymes addressed themselves by select messengers unto Nicholas Jacson of Hibaldstow to admonish him of his remissness & careless walking in the way of Truth & holyness, and to exhort him to return unto the Lord and to his everlasting Truth from whome & from whence he is departed, and finding the said Nicholas from time to time to evade such admonitions and councells as have been given him, not answering the expectations of Friends in any of their friendly addresses. It is by generall consent of Freinds determined & adjudged, that Friends are clear of the bloud

[1] 10th January, 1677.

of the said Nicholas Jackson, seeing he hath refused to returne at their reproofs & counsells, and they doe in the dread & feare of the Lord leave him to the righteous judgement of God, who will render unto every man according to his works.

Thomas Thorowgate of Hibaldstow & Hannah Potter of Lea came this day the second time into the Monthly Meeting both of them signifying their intentions to marry each other and Friends of this meeting having found all things faire & cleare betwixt them have given their assent, & left the Consummation of their said marriage to their own conveniency according to the good order of Truth.

The next Monthly Meeting to be at the house of Thomas Wresle at Boterwick.

p. 65.

At a Monthly Meeting of Friends held at the house of Thomas Wresle of Boterwick the fourteenth day of the twelth month 1676[1] :—

It is desired that Henry Sympson & Peter Naylor goe as messengers from this Meeting unto Thomas Taylor of Gainsborough to know why he did not meet Friends this day at their request, and also to desire him the second tyme to be present at the next Monthly Meeting.

It is ordered that both the contributions be collected and brought in to the next Monthly Meeting.

The next Meeting to be at the house of Robert Ashton in Ealand.

To Robert Everatt, John Urry & Henry Hudson & to all other who refraine meeting with Friends at the house of Michael Monkton in Beltoft.

Deare Friends

Wee whose names are hereunder written being met together in the name of our Lord Jesus Christ, in our Monthly Meeting upon the service of the Truth being advertised that severall of you doe separate & absent your selves from the Unity of Friends in your Perticuler Meeting at such tyme as by order it falls out to be at the house of Michael Monkton, upon occasion of some offence taken against him, whilst yet you have made no complaint thereof unto this Monthly Meeting, although thereto desired. now, we doe with our heart, in the feare of God, desire you not to forsake the assembly of the Lords people, at such time as the Meeting by due course falls to be at his house, untill your complaint hath been made to the Monthly Meeting (and Michael have liberty to answere for himselfe) who will doe all things according to justice & righteousnes ; in the meantime we agains (in the bowels of brotherly love) desire and admonish you,

[1] 14th February, 1677.

not to absent your selves, neither lay a stumbling block before the feet of your weake brethren to cause them to fall, untill this matter may be proceeded in according to the good order of Truth.

Thomas Markham
John Bennyson[1]
Thomas Wresle of Wintringham
Edmond Morley
Peter Naylor
Thomas Wresle of Boterwick
Joseph Pacey
Christopher Edwards
Robert Rockhill
Robert Collier

p. 66.

At a Monthly Meeting of Friends held the fourteenth day of the 1st month 1676/7[2] :—

brought in of the contribution generall		£	s.	d.
	Boterwick ..	0	18	00
	Garthrope ..	0	13	04
	Winteringham ..	1	1	0
	Gainsburgh ..	0	15	0
	Brigg	1	1	0
		4	8	4
Contribution particular				
	Crowle	0	18	0
	Garthrope ..	0	13	4
	Wintringam ..	0	17	5
	Gainsburgh ..	0	14	0
	Brigg	0	18	6
		4	1	3
Returnd back to the severall meetings				
	Wintringham ..	0	5	0
	Garthrup ..	0	4	0
	Boterwick ..	0	5	0
	Brigg	0	1	3
		0	15	3
	Remaining ..	3	6	0

The next Monthly Meeting to be at the house of Robert Ashton in Ealand.

[1] *sic recte* Benington. [2] 14th March, 1677.

p. 67.

At a Monthly Meeting of Friends held at the house of Robert Ashton of Ealand the eleventh day of the 2d month 1677[1] :—

Whereas Henry Sympson & Peter Naylor were by the Monthly Meeting held at Thomas Wresles at Boterwick the 14th day of the 12th month 1676, to speak to Thomas Tayler and to desire his presence at this Meeting that he might then & there know & feele the love & tendernes of Friends to his soule, and they faileing to bring or send an account of their said service at this time, therefore it is the desire of Friends of this meeting that William West put Henry Sympson & Peter Nayler in mind of their duty, that they perform it effectually the next Monthly Meeting.

This day Henry Hudson only, came to this meeting in order to fulfill the letter of Friends sent to him & others, concerning a complaint to be by them made against Michael Monkton of Beltoft, and saith that on a tyme when Michael Monkton was newly come from London, he the said Henry went to him gave the hand & asked how he did, to which Michael replied "You are all nought".

It is desired by Friends of this Monthly Meeting, that all such Freinds who absent from Meetings at Michael Monktons house (or would have them discontinued there) would come to the next Monthly Meeting and give unto Friends an account of what matters & things they have to lay to his charge, that Friends may proceed therein according to the good order of Truth, and Thomas Wresle of Boterwick is desired to give all such Friends as are concernd. notice of it.

This day Nathaneel Nainby & Anne Odlin both of Brigg came into this meeting & acquainted them with their purpose of marriage which Friends have taken into consideration till the next Monthly Meeting.

The next Meeting to be at the house of Thomas Wresle in Boterwick.

At a Monthly Meeting of Friends held at the house of Thomas Wresle of Boterwick the 9th day 3d month 1677[2] :—

This day Nathaneel Naineby of Glamford Briggs came the second time into the Monthly Meeting signifying his intentions to marry Anne Odlin of the same, and Friends finding all things faire & cleare betwixt them, have given their assent, and left the consumation thereof to their own conveniency according to the good order of Truth.

The next Monthly Meeting to be at Gainsburgh.

[1] 11th April, 1677. [2] 9th May, 1677.

p. 68.

Att a Monthly Meeting held att Gainsburgh the 13 of 4th month 1677[1] :—

Contributions came in as followeth

	£	s.	d.
Gainsburgh	00	18	02
Epworth ..	01	11	00
Garthorpe ..	00	18	00
Winteringam	01	07	00
Brigg ..	01	13	09
	6	07	11

Returnd to Thomas Wresle; 7*s.* 11*d.* Reste 6*l.* to goe to the next Quarterly Meeting.

It is ordered that Thomas Wresle & Robert Ashton goe from this meeting & advise Edward Cheesman to putt a speedy end to the differnse betwixt himselfe & his neighbour & bring in his answer the next Monthly Meeting.

It is ordered that the next Monthly Meeting be att Adlingfleet att the house of Edward[2] Morley :

Att a Monthly Meeteing held att Adlinfleete the 11th day of the 5th moneth 1677[3] :—

Christopher Wilson & Edmond Morley are appointed by this Meeteing, to speake to & advise Edward Chessman to put an end to the difference betwixt his neighbour & himselfe, & bringe his answer to the next Monthly Meeteing.

Its ordered that the next Monethly Meeteing be att the house of Thomas Wreasle in Boterweeke.

p. 69.

At a Monthly Meeting held att Buterwick att Thomas Wresels the 8th of the 6th month 1677[4] :—

The next Monthly Metting to be att the house of Thomas Markham in Brigg.

Att a Monthly Meeting held at the house of Thomas Markham in Brigg the 12th 7 ber 1677[5] :—

	£	s.	d.
Gainsbrough	00	13	9
Epworth	00	19	8
Garthorp	00	14	6
Wintringham	00	19	9
Brigg	01	06	6
	04	14	02

[1] 13th June, 1677. [2] *sic recte* Edmond. [3] 11th July, 1677.
[4] 8th August, 1677. [5] 12th September, 1677.

Disbursments

to Gainsbrough meeting	00 : 06 : 06
to Epworth meeting ..	00 : 05 : 00
to Brigg Meeting ..	00 : 05 : 00
	00 : 16 : 06

sent up to the Quarterly Meeting.. 03 : 17 : 8

This day William Cam came into the Monthly Meeting & did publish his intentions of marriage with Elizabeth Haslaby and did alsoe bring a certificate from the Monthly Meeting at Blyth and relations being satisfied as by certificates undr there hand doth appear it is left to the consideration of Freinds of Blyth Monthly Meeting.

This day a writeing was sent from this Monthly Meeting to Edward Chessman once more to desire him to put an end to the difference betwixt him & his neighbour, otherwise the Meeting doth intend to withdraw from him as one that walks disorderly, and Thomas Wresle & Robert Ashton is desired to deliver the said writeing & bring his answer to the next Monthly Meeting.

p. 70.

It is ordered that the next Monthly Meeting be att Robert Ashton house in Ealand.

Att a Monthly Metting held the 10th day of the eight month 77 att Robert Ashtons house in Ealand[1] :—

The difference betwext Edward Chesman and his neighbour is ended according to Friends desire.

It is ordered that the next Monthly Meetting be att Thomas Wresle's house in Butterweicke.

Att a Monthly Meeting held att the house of Thomas Wresle in Butterwick 14 : 9th month 1677[2] :—

Whereas William Camm of Gainsburgh came some meetings since to the Monthly Meeting to declare his intentions of marryage with Elizabeth Hasleby this meeting doth declare they have nothing against the said marryage butt they are left to Gainsburgh Meeting & North Clay Meeting to perfect the Matter :

It is ordered that generall Contribution be maid throughout all the Monthly Meeting according to the order of the Quarterly Meeting & brought in to the next Monthly Meeting.

It is ordered that the next Monthly Meeting be held att the house of Thomas Markham of Brigg :

[1] 10th October, 1677.

[2] 14th November, 1677.

p. 71.

Att a Monthly Meeting held att the house of Thomas Markhams house in Brigg the 10: Xth month 77[1] :—

Contribucions came in as follows:

		£	s.	d.
Gainsburgh	..	00	14	07
Brigg ..	..	01	01	00
Winteringham	..	01	01	00
Epworth	..	01	03	06
Garthorpe	..	00	13	00½
		4	13	01½

Retornd to Epworth 10*s.*
To Winteringam 3*s.* 1*d*½.

Ordered the some of 4*l.* to goe up to the Quarterly Meeting att Lyncolne.

It is ordered that the next Monthly Meeting be held att the house of Thomas Markham in Brigg.

Francis Cooke of East Hawton belonging to this Meeting did att the said Meeting declare his intentions to take to wife Judith Groyser (shee present) of the same place & they was desired by the said Meeting to stay untill next Monthly Meeting that enquiry might be maid whether all things was cleare that Truth might not suffer.

At a Monthly Meeting held at the house of Thomas Markham in Brigg the 9th day 11th month 77[2] :—

This day Francis Cook of East Halton came the second time into the Monthly Meetting signifying his intentions to marry Judith Grosyer of the same & Freinds haveing nothing against it, have given there assent, & left the consumation thereof to there own conveniency, according to the good order of Truth.

It is ordered that the next Monthly Meetting be at the house of Thomas Wresle in Butterwick.

p. 72.

At a Monthly Meeting at the house of Thomas Wresle in West Butterwick the 13 day of the 12 month 77/8[3] :—

It is ordered that John Hallewell be with Mathew Tranmore untill the next Monthly Meeting and the said Meeting is to see him satisfied in the meantime Thomas Markham is ordred to speak to Vincent Brownlow to see if he will take him to his trade & to send his answer to the next Monthly Meeting.

[1] 10th December, 1677. [2] 9th January, 1678. [3] 13th February, 1678.

It is ordered that a contribution be collected and brought in to the next Monthly Meeting.

It is ordered that the next Monthly Meeting be at the house of Thomas Markham in Brigg.

Att a Monthly Meeting at the house of Thomas Markham in Brigg the 13 day of 1st Month 1677/8[1] :—

Contributions as followeth

	£	s.	d.
Gainsbrough	00 :	13 :	04
Epworth	00 :	16 :	04
Wintringham	00 :	18 :	04
Garthorp	00 :	13 :	03
Brigg	01 :	03 :	00
	04 :	04 :	03
disbursed to the severall Meeting	01 :	04 :	03
sent up to the Quarterly Meeting	03 :	00 :	00

An agreement made with Robert Wilkinson of Wintringham by the Monthly Meeting the said Robert is to take William Hallewell an apprentice to learn the trade of a weaver he is to take him with nothing and the Meeting is to find him all necessaryes for seaven years beginning the 25 instant.

It is ordred that the next Monthly Meeting be held at the house of Robert Ashton in Ealand.

p. 73.

10 day 2d Month 1678[2]

Att a Monthly Meeting att the house of Robert Ashton in Ealand whereas a differance is depending betwixt George Nicholson and Joseph Pope it is conclewded that all diferances shall be refarred to Robert Rukell and Laton Firbank if they two cannott agree them then the two referrees to chewes a third man to make a finall end of all differances what ever.

It is ordered that the next Monthly Meeteing be held att the house of John Wressell in Thelby.

At a Monthly Metinge helde at the house of John Wresell in Thelby the eight day of the third month 1678[3] :—

That the difrance betwixte George Nickllson and Joseph Pope which was refard to Robert Ruckill and Laton Furbank is ended as farr as Frinds are concernd the reste lefte to the owners of the farms.

[1] 13th March, 1678. [2] 10th April, 1678. [3] 8th May, 1678.

It is ordred that the next Monthly Metinge be helld at the house of Henery Simson at Gainsboro and that a contrybucion be then brout in.

Att a Monthly Meeting at the house of Henery Simson in Gainsbrough the 12 day of the 4th Month 78[1] :—

Contributions as followeth

	£	s.	d.
Gainsbrough	00	13	06
Epworth	01	01	10
Winteringham	00	17	04
Garthorpe	00	13	00
Brigg	01	00	00
	4	5	8

p. 74.

Disbursments out of the contributions as followeth

	£	s.	d.
To Willy West	2	10	0
To Henery Sympson: towards the nursing of	1	0	0
Mary Codd and Apprall	0	3	3
To Henery Sympson for the paying of a poore Friends rent	0	4	6
To Thomas Wresle of Butterwick for a poore Friends Rent	0	7	11
	4	5	8

This day Joseph Pacye & Prisseley Parker came to this Meeting & did publish there intentions of marriage & we have taken it in to consideration untill the next Monthly Meeting.

It is desired that some woemen Friends be at the next Quarterly Meeting from every particular Meeting.

And that the next Monthly Meeting be at Adlinfleet at the house of Christopher Wilson.

the 12th day of the 4th month : 78[1].

Received then of Friends of the Monthly Meeting the some of seaven pounds & ten shillings being in full satisfaction for the bringing up of Rebeckah Codd for the tearme of ten yeares. I say Received by me . . . William West. 07 : 10 : 00

p. 75.

Att a Monthly Meeting at the house of Christopher Wilson in Adlinfleet the 10th day of 5th month 1678[2] :—

By a writeing from the Quarterly Meeting held at Lincoln the 26 of the 4th Month[3] it was ordred that two Freinds in every

[1] 12th June, 1678. [2] 10th July, 1678. [3] 26th June, 1678.

particular Meeting be made choice of by the Monthly Meeting to take an account of all the sufferings that may happen in there respective Meetings & especially that of tythes taken from Freinds by priests or impropriators with out their consent & a true record to be made of all such sufferings & brought up to the Monthly Meeting.

For Gainsbrough Meeting William Garland, Henry Simson

For Crowle Meeting Thomas Wresle Robert Ashton

Garthorp Meeting, Robert Reeder Christopher Wilson

Wintringham Meeting Thomas Wresle Anthony Westaby

Brigg Meeting Robert Rockhill Thomas Markham

Joseph Pacye came the second time into the Monthly Meeting signifying his intentions of marriage with Prisselley Parker now of Pollington & hath brought a certificate from the Monthly Meeting at Sike House that they have made due publication in that Meeting and all things being found clear both with them and alsoe with us the consummation thereof is left to themselves at there best convenience.

It is ordred that Georg Nicholson appear at the next Monthly Meeting to prove his charg against John Whitehead Robert Rockhill Thomas Wresle John Hogg & others and Thomas Wressle of Wintringham & William Herrison of the same is to signifie it accordingly. It is alsoe desired that Robert Reeder appear there alsoe & Christopher Wilson is to give him notice of it.

It is concluded that the next Monthly Meeting be held at the house of Thomas Markham in Brigg.

p. 76.

Att a Monthly Meeting held att Brigg the 14: day of the 6th month 1678[1] :—

It is concluded that the severall Freinds mencond the last Monthly Meeting concerning the sufferings of Freinds per Tiths or other Sufferings be dilligent in bringing an account of the same to the next Monthly Meeting.

It is ordered that there be generall contribucon maid throughout all the Meetings belonging to this Monthly Meeting & brought in to the next Monthly Meeting.

It is ordered that Vincent Brownely take to apprentice John Hallywell & his tyme to begin the first of the 3d month last & to receive 40*s.*: per yeare for the first foure yeares & 40*s.* per Annum for the 3 last yeares to be alsoe putt into Vincents pleasure to take it if he please.

[1] 14th August, 1678.

It is ordered that the next Monthly Meeting be at the house of Henry Simsons in Gainsbrough.

p. 77.

Att a Monthly Meeting held at the house of Thomas Markham in Brigg the 14th 6th month 1678[1] :—

Whereas it was ordred the last Monthly Meeting that George Nicholson should appear at the abovesaid Monthly Meeting to make good such charges & reflections given against John Whitehead Robert Rockhill Thomas Wresle John Hogge & others in a case of difference betwixt Joseph Pope & the said Georg Nicholson which was finally concluded by the said John Whitehead Robert Rockhill Thomas Wresle & John Hogg &c and upon the full hearing of the case it is apparent to this Meeting that the said Georg hath manifestly erred from the Truth in his severe charges against Freinds concerned seeking to extenuate his fault by denying severall things plainly proved against him as alsoe in refuseing the tender admonitions of such Freinds in not being willing to give a plaine & full condemnation against that spirit that soe acted him but rather still agravateing by more reflections & excuseing of himselfe for which causes this meeting beleeve it there duty to condemn that spirit by which in the things abovesaid he was acted and they doe hereby condemn it and cannot have unity with him untill he as publickly condemn the same.

William Smith
William Williamson
Thomas Markham
Robert Collier
Christopher Wilson
John Odlin
Joseph Richardson
Robert Scott
William Garland
William West
Vincent Brownlow
Edward Gilliat
Anthony Westoby
Henry Simpson

p. 78.

At a Monthly Meeting held at the house of Henry Simson in Gainsbrough the 11 7ber 1678[2] :—

Contributions as followeth

	£	s.	d.
Gainsbrough Meeting ..	00 :	11 :	10
Wintringham Meeting ..	00 :	17 :	00
Brigg Meeting ..	01 :	00 :	06
Garthorp Meeting ..	00 :	13 :	06
Epworth Meeting ..	01 :	00 :	02
	04 :	03 :	00

[1] 14th August, 1678. [2] 11th September, 1678.

	£	s.	d.
Disbursements out of the Contribution paid to Henry Simson toward the nursing of Christopher Codd Child	01 :	00 :	00
Sent back to Garthorp	00 :	06 :	8
Paid by Henry Simson for discharg of Thomas Peel his rent the sum of	00 :	10 :	00
Paid to Thomas Markham laid down by him ..	00 :	02 :	6
	01 :	19 :	2
Sent up to the Quarterly Meeting	02 :	03 :	10
Money from the Quarterly Meeting to be added ..		15 :	00
totall	02 :	18 :	10

Wheras we have received an account that Peter Moody hath contrary to the order of Truth and to the weakning of the testimony of faithfull Freinds hath from time to time paid tyths notwithstanding the councell & advice of Freinds to the contrary, it is therefore ordred by this Monthly Meeting that Thomas Wresle and Robert Scott admonish him to return to the Truth which doth condemn all such practices and to bring in his answer to the next Monthly Meeting.

p. 79.

This Meeting hath again taken into consideration the condition of Thomas Taylor of Gainsbrough and though he hath often rejected the advice of Freinds sent to him from this Meeting yet if soe be ther may be hope concerning him it is desired that he be once more admonished to return to the Truth & alsoe to give in his answer himselfe at the next Monthly Meeting and Robert Everatt is desired to speak to him accordingley.

Wheras it was ordred by a Monthly Meeting the eleaventh day of the 2d Month 1677 held at the house of Robert Ashtons in Ealand that severall Freinds viz Robert Everatt John Urry Henry Hudson &c did absent themselves from the unity of Freinds in ther particular meeting when by due course it did fall at the house of Michaell Monkton that the said Robert Everat & John Urry & Henry Hudson &c should come to the next Monthly Meeting and shew there reasons of soe doeing & Thomas Wresle of Butterwick was desired to give them notice thereof now ther being noe answer recorded it is desired by this meeting for the clearing of the Truth that Thomas Wresle give in ther answer to the next Meeting.

It is concluded that the next Monthly Meeting be at the house of Thomas Wresle in Butterwick.

p. 80.

At a Monthly Meeting held at the house of Thomas Wresles in West Butterwick the 9th day of the 8th month 1678[1] :—

Whereas there was a complaint made against Peter Moody the last Monthly Meeting that the said Peter from time to time did pay tythes, now he being spoaken to by Thomas Wresle doth confess that once he did give way that the impropriator should take them but did acknowledg he had therein acted contrary to Truth in his own conscience & did hope he should not doe the like any more.

Wheras Robert Everat was desired by this Meeting once more to exhort Thomas Taylor to return to the Truth from which it is manifest he is departed And this answer he hath returned vid : that he takes noe notice of our advice or councell, & said that he would not come to the dore to speak with any of us, soe that haveing long sought after him in the spirit of meekness we doe judge this Meeting is clear of him & doe hereby declare we have noe unity with that spirit which acts in him & soe he is left to the consideration of the Quarterly Meeting.

Wheras it was ordred the last Monthly Meeting that Thomas Wresle of Butterwick should give an account to this Meeting of the answer of Robert Everatt, John Urry, Henry Hudson &c wherfore they absented themselves from there particular Meeting when by due course it fell to be at the house of Michael Monkton, and the said Thomas Wresle gives this in as ther answer : that the said Freinds were willing at the desire of this meeting to continue the said Meeting & severall of them did soe accordingly, but the abovesaid M : Monkton very shortly removeing his family that Meeting fell of itselfe and that which was an offence to the abovesaid Freinds in M : Monkton was by that means taken out of the way.

It is concluded that the next Monthly Meeting be at the house of Robert Scott in Crowle.

p. 81.

At a Monthly Meeting held att the house of Robert Scott of Crowle the 13th day of the 9th moneth 1678[2] :—

At the Meeting abovesaid ; from the Meeting att Winteringham we are informed that whereas heretofore ther hath bene some controversy betwixt John Johnson of Burton and John Dent of Thealby (boath being members of the said Meeting ;) which hath occationed the breach of that brotherly Love which ought to be held & practised amongst Christian brethren And the Perticuler Meeting to which they belong having labored

[1] 9th October, 1678. [2] 13th November, 1678.

to reconcile the same: yet finding there labor of love and Christian practice performed by them not to effect what was desired & labored for: But that upon new provocations it appears they are not heartyly reconsiled each to other: And whereas a new difference being of late falen out betwixt the said John Johnson & John Dent: That Meting to whome thay belonge doe desire the assistance of the next Monethly Meeting to heare and detirmine the matter of difference betwixt them: That if possible all rancor and bitterness may be donn away; and brotherly love possess boath of there hearts each to other And this Monethly Meeting doth desire Thomas Wresle & Will Harrison to give notice to the said Freinds to bring in what thay have against each other to the next Monthly Meeting.

It is allso ordered the day and year abovesaid that a contribution be maid in every perticuler Meeting belonging to this Monethly Meeting and brought in to the next.

It is allsoe ordered that the next Monethly Meeting be held att the house of John Wressell att Thealby.

THE 11TH 10TH MONTH 1678[1] :—

Whearas John Dent & John Johnson was desired to appear at this Meeting to lay open some matters of differences that had happened betwixt them and to refer it to the said meeting this may sattisfie whome it may concern that the abovesaid John Dent & John Johnson did appear accordingly and this Meeting have judged them both to have erred from the Truth and in the love of God have admonished them to return to the truth which admonishon they did receive and have from the heart forgiven one another, and promised for the time to come to walk inoffencively toward each other.

John Dent
John Johnson

p. 82.

ATT a Monthly Meeting held at the house of John Wresles in Thealby the 11th of 10th month 1678[2] :—

Contributions brought in as followeth

	£	s.	d.
Crowle Meeting ..	00	17	01
Brigg Meeting	00	18	00
Garthorp Meeting ..	00	13	03
Wintringham Meeting..	00	16	10
Gainsbrough Meeting ..	00	12	07
	03	17	09

[1] 11th December, 1678. [2] 11th December, 1678.

			£	s.	d.
Disbursments	Crowle Meeting	..	01	05	00
	Gainsbrough Meeting	..	01	11	08
			02	16	8
Sent up to the Quarterly Meeting from this Meeting			02	19	4

The next Monthly Meeting is to be held at the house of Thomas Markham in Brigg.

Att a Monthly Meetting held at the house of Thomas Markham in Brigg the 8th day of the 11th month 1678[1] :—

no business appearing

It is ordered the next Monthly Meetting be held at the house of Thomas Wresle in West Buterwick.

Att a Monthly Meetting held at the house of Thomas Wresle in Butterwick the 12th of the 12th month 1678[2] :—

Whereas a paper was ordred to be read in this Monthly Meeting which was sent by Robert Rockhill to the said Meeting and there being some thing in the said paper not soe well understood. It is ordered by this Meeting that Robert Rockhill appear at the next Monthly Meeting to give his sence of his own writeing.

p. 83.

It is ordered that a contribution be collected & brought in to the next Monthly Meeting.

It is ordered that the next Monthly Meeting be held at the house of Thomas Markham in Brigg.

Att a Monthly Meeting held at the house of Thomas Markham the 12 of the First month 1678/9[3] :—

This day Robert Rockhill was present at the Monthly Meeting and did satisfy Friends in what they desired concerning his written page, according to the order abovesaid.

Whereas it is reported to this Meeting that Robert Everat hath taken some occation against Robert Scott & Thomas Wresle in somuch as he doth not only forbear to assemble with Freinds of that Meeting but alsoe hath denyed Freinds the liberty of his house to meet in when by due course it falls there, it is therefore ordered by this Meeting that Henry Simson & John Pilsworth speak to him that he make his appearance at the next Monthly Meeting & shew the grounds of his dissatisfaction, and the above said Henry Simson & John Pilsworth is orderd to speak to Robert Scott & Thomas Wresle that they appear at the said Meeting to answer to such things as shall by the said Robert be charged against them.

[1] 8th January, 1679. [2] 12th February, 1679. [3] 12th March, 1679.

Contributions		£	s.	d.
	Brigg Meeting	00	17	06
	Crowle Meeting ..	01	03	00
	Garthorp Meeting ..	00	14	00
	Gainsbrough Meeting ..	00	13	08
	Wintringham Meeting..	00	15	03
		04	03	05
Money remaining in stock in the hands of Thomas Markham		1	11	04
		5	14	9
Returnd back to Wintringham		00	05	6
Returnd back to Gainsbrough		01	15	9
Returnd to Butterwick Meeting		00	06	0
To Garthorp meeting		00	04	6
To Brigg meeting		00	03	0
		02	14	9
Sent up to the Quarterly Meeting		03	00	00

p. 84.

Whereas a complaint hath been made by severall Freinds belonging to Hull Meeting against Edward Chesman of Belton that the said Edward doth refuse to pay three pounds a year according to an agreement made upon a certain sum of moneys in hand paid to him unto widdow Law his wife's Mother. Thomas Wresle & Robert Ashton is ordred by this Meeting to speak to the said Edward to know wherfore he doth refuse to pay the abovesaid sum according to agreement and to bring his answer to the next Monthly Meeting.

It is ordred that the next Monthly Meeting be at the house of John Pilsworth in Epworth the 3d fourth day in the next Month because the Quarterly Meeting falls the same day when the Monthly by course should be.

At a Monthly Meeting held at Epworth the 16 day of the 2d month 1679[1] :—

Whereas the preceding Monthly Meeting did order Henry Sympson & John Pilsworth to speak to Robert Everatt about some difference between him & some other Freinds of Crowle meeting, they have spoken unto him accordingly and that business is composed, and all freinds at difference reconciled, and remaine in the unity of the Truth.

Whereas (upon the request of Friends of Hull Monthly Meeting) Thomas Wresle & Robert Ashton were ordered by this Meeting to speak to Edward Chessman, about some unfair dealing

[1] 16th April, 1679.

with his mother in law, & to bring his answere to this meeting which is that Edward hath promised to goe to Hull very shortly after the tyme called Easter and give them satisfaction.

Ordered that a few lines be sent to Hull Meeting to give them an account of his answer.

Ordered that a contribution be collected & brought in to the next Monthly Meeting which is ordered to be at the house of Robert Ashton in Ealand.

Signed in the name & by appointment of this Meeting

Robert Rockhill

p. 85.

Att a Monthly Meeting held at Ealand the 14th day of the 3rd month 1679[1] :—

No further business appearing it is ordered that the next Monthly Meeting be held at the house of Henry Sympson in Gainsburgh.

At a Monthly Meeting held at Gainsbrough the 11th day of the 4th month 1679[2] :—

Ordered that William Garland & Henry Sympson & Peter Naylor be impowered to treat and agree with Anne Reckett about the tuition of Mary the daughter of Christopher Codd late deceased and to give an account of their agreement to the next Monthly Meeting.

Whereas formerly (upon Complaint of Hull Friends unto this Meeting, against Edward Chessman of Belton for some wrong done to his mother in law) two Friends were ordered by this meeting to speak with him about it and return his answere. which was that he would shortly goe to Hull and give them satisfaction, but having not yet performed his promise, process at law is issued out against him, to the great scandall of the Truth, for the prevention whereof, or at least the further spreading of it, this meeting hath ordered Thomas Wresle of Boterwick & Robert Ashton to admonish Edward Chessman to make a speedy agreement with his mother in law, and give a finall conclusion to that difference, and bring a certificate from some of Hull Friends that he hath done soe, before the next monthly Meeting for these parts otherwise Friends of this meeting will be constrained to proceed against him (as a transgressor) according to the good order of Truth.

This day Robert Vessey of Belton and Joan Marshall of Luddington came into this Meeting, and declared their purpose of marriage each with other and (being the first time) Freinds have taken it into consideration, and desired them to wait till the next Monthly Meeting, where they are both desired to be present.

[1] 14th May, 1679. [2] 11th June, 1679.

Contributions from :	Gainsburgh ..	00 : 19 : 00	returned to :	00 : 01 : 01
	Brigge ..	01 : 02 : 00		00 : 02 : 00
	Garthorpe ..	00 : 15 : 00		
	Crowle ..	01 : 01 : 08		00 : 09 : 00
	Winteringham	01 : 13 : 01		
	totall ..	05 : 10 : 09		00 : 12 : 01

To be sent up to the Quarterly Meeting 04 : 18 : 08

Ordered that the next Meeting be at the house of Robert Reeder in Garthorpe.

Signed in the name & by appointment of this Meeting

Robert Rockhill

p. 86.

At a Monthly Meeting held in the house of Robert Reeder att Garthorpe the 9th day of the 5th month 1679[1] :—

In pursuance of the order of the last Monthly Meeting, William Garland, Henry Sympson & Peter Naylor recount unto this meeting that Anne Reckett demandeth seaven pounds with Mary Codd, in consideration whereof she is willing to acquitt Friends from all further charge, and take the child in the condition she is at present and keep her eight years, or till she shall be aged 18 yeares, now it is by this Meeting ordered that William Garland, Henry Sympson & Peter Naylor doe conclude with Anne Reckett upon her own conditions, provided they take two years tyme for the payment of the mony, at severall payments, that is to say 40*s* in each half year for the first 3 halfe years, and 20*s* for the last. Conditioned also that in case Anne Reckett shall dye within one yeare after the last payment, some reasonable part of the mony be repaid unto this Meeting.

In pursuance of another order of the last Monthly Meeting Thomas Wresle & Robert Ashton give this meeting this account that Edward Chessman assures them he hath ended the difference betwixt him and his mother in law, and did shew them 2 acquitances for the severall sums of mony in controversy, with which account this meeting is satisfyed at the present.

Robert Vessey of Belton & Joan Marshall of Luddington came into this meeting the second time, and declared the continuance of their purpose of marriage, and Friends having nothing against it, but finding all things clear, have left the consummation thereof to their own conveniency according to the good order of Truth.

[1] 9th July, 1679.

	s.	d.
Ordered that Gainsburgh Friends give an account of the contribution sent up to Lincolne there wanting	13 :	2

The next Meeting ordered to be at the house of Thomas Markham in Brigge,

Signed Robert Rockhill

p. 87.

At a Monthly Meeting held at Glamford Bridge the 13th day of the 6th month 1679[1] :—

This day Henry Hudson of West Boterwick and Helene Kelsey of Epworth came into this meeting and declared their purpose of marriage each with other, and being the first tyme Friends have taken it into consideration, and desire them to wait till the next Monthly Meeting where they both are desired to be present.

s. d.
The 13 : 2 wanting in the last contribution sent to Lincolne was paid to Anne Reckett for the keeping of Mary Codd till midsomer as Friends of Gainsburgh meeting give account.

The next Meeting ordered at Thomas Wresles in West Boterwick.

Signed Robert Rockhill

At a Monthly Meeting held at Boterwick the 10th day of the 7th month 1679[2] :—

This day Henry Hudson and Helene Kelsey came the second tyme into this Meeting expecting the answer of Friends to their purpose of marriage mentioned the last Monthly Meeting; who finding all things clear, have left the consummation thereof to their own conveniency, provided Friends of that Meeting see to the settlement of a certain house upon the child of William Kelsey her first husband, before the marriage be finished.

Friends of this Monthly Meeting having long waited for George Nicholson's repentance, and returning to the Unity of Friends in the Truth, and finding no good fruit thereof, in pursuance of their duty on truths behalfs, have written to him as followeth :

George Nicholson

It is now more then twelve months since upon a free debate & full hearing of thy case, Friends of that Monthly Meeting passed true judgement therein. In all which time they have waited to

[1] 13th August, 1679. [2] 10th September, 1679.

see the good effects thereof produced by thee to witt, a filiall shame and godly sorrow for all such thy disorders as have occasioned that censure. But contrarywise Friends find thee exalted in thy mind, not only refusing to submitt to true judgement aforesaid but also taking upon thee to preach and pray in the Meetings of the Lords people, while thou art yet unreconciled to the brethren; which practice may in no wise be suffered, being so directly repugnant to the doctrine of our Lord Jesus Christ. Matthew 5.23.24. Wherefore, wee being met together in his naime in our Monthly Meeting at Boterwick, in true love to thy soule admonish thee (as thou tenders the glory of God, and thine own eternall peace) to descend those dangerous degrees whereby thou art exalted. Consider what thou hast done and be ashamed. Lay thy hand upon thy heart and humble thy selfe before the Lord, if so be thou maist find mercy. And when that is done, and thou truly reconciled to thy brethren then thou maist offer thy gift.

Crowle ..	01 : 00 : 06	Returnd back ..	00 : 10 : 08
Wintringham..	00 : 18 : 03	more to Vincent	
Garthrope ..	00 : 13 : 00	Brownlow for..	00 : 12 : 00
Brigge ..	00 : 18 : 00	John Hallywell	
Added by T.M.	00 : 11 : 05		
Gainsburgh to be added		To be sent to Lincolne	02 : 18 : 00

William Garland gave an account to this Meeting that the agreement with Anne Reckett for the keeping of Mary Codd is concluded.

The next Monthly Meeting ordered to be att Brigge:

Signed R. Rockhill

p. 88.

At a Monthly Meeting held at Brigge the 8th day 8th month 1679[1]:—

This day Friends of Gainsburgh Meeting sent in their agreement with Anne Reckett about Mary Codd, which is recorded as followeth

Memorandum, it is agreed the eighth day of the 7th Month 1679[2] Between Friends of Gainsburgh Meeting of the one part, And Anne Reckett of Gate Burton in the County of Lincolne: of the other parte. That for the consideration of seaven pounds & ten shillings to be paid by this Monthly Meeting in two years time unto Anne Reckett, the said Anne doth hereby covenant to take Mary the daughter of Christopher Codd late deceased, and her to keep from the time called midsomer last before the date hereof, until she shall attain the age of eighteen years. Finding and

[1] 8th October, 1679. [2] 8th September, 1679.

providing unto the said Mary dureing all the said terme sufficient meat, drink & apparrell with lodging and all other things necessary both for life & health. And if it shall happen the said Anne Reckett to dye within twelve months after the payment of the aforesd sum: of 07*l.* : 10*s.* : 00 She doth hereby for her selfe her executors & administrators covenant & grant to pay back the summe of forty shillings unto Friends of Gainsburgh Meeting, or whome they shall appoint.

In the presence of
William West
Mary Boole

Sealed & Signed
Anne Reckett

The next Meeting appointed to be at the house of Thomas Wresle in Boterwick.

Signed R. Rockhill

AT a Monthly Meeting held at Boterwick the 12 day 9th month 1679[1] :—

Complaint being made this day by a neighbour of Boterwick against Edward Chessman for some unequall proceedings with him; this meeting hath appointed Thomas Wresle & Henry Hudson to discourse Edward Chessman about the truth of the Complaint, and give account thereof to the next Monthly Meeting.

Ordred that a contribution be collected throughout all the meetings belonging to this Monthly, and brought in to the next Monthly Meeting, whence Friends necessityes being supplyed, the rest to be carryed to the Quarterly Meeting.

Ordred that Thomas Wresle of Boterwick desire John Robinson of Epworth as from this meeting, to be present att the next Monthly Meeting, for that Friends desire to speak with him. The next Meeting ordered to be att Brigge.

Signed Robert Rockhill

p. 89.

AT a Monthly Meeting held at the house of Thomas Markham in Brigge the tenth day of the tenth month 1679[2] :—

	In stock	01 : 02 : 06
	Gainsburgh	00 : 10 : 10
	Brigg	00 : 17 : 00
Contributions brought in	Crowle	00 : 13 : 08
	Garthorpe	00 : 12 : 06
	Wintringham	00 : 16 : 06
	Totall ..	04 : 13 : 00

[1] 12th November, 1679. [2] 10th December, 1679.

	Gainsburgh to Anne Reckett for Mary Codd	01 : 00 : 00
	Brigg	00 : 07 : 00
returnd	Crowle	00 : 10 : 00
unto	Garthorpe	00 : 05 : 00
	Wintringham for William Hallywell	00 : 15 : 04
	totall ..	03 : 07 : 04
To be sent up the Quarterly Meeting		01 : 05 : 00

Thomas Wresle & Henry Hudson recount unto this Meeting that the difference between Edward Chesman & his neighbour of Boterwick is ended, and John Robinson of Epworth desires respite untill the Meeting fall neerer to his dwelling:

The next Meeting appointed to be at Brigg.

Signed R. Rockhill

At a Monthly Meeting held at the house of Thomas Markham in Brigg the fourteenth day of the Eleventh month 1679[1] :—

Ordered that a contribution for the supply of Friends necessityes be forthwith collected throughout the severall Meetings & brought in to the next Monthly Meeting, which is appointed at the house of Thomas Wresle in Boterwick.

Signed R. Rockhill

At a Monthly Meeting held at the house of Thomas Wresle in Boterwick the eleventh day of the twelth month 1679[2] :—

Crowle	00 : 18 : 09
Gainsburgh	00 : 11 : 02
Wintringham	00 : 18 : 10
Garthorpe	00 : 14 : 00
Brigge	00 : 18 : 06
	04 : 01 : 03
Returned back to Crowle	00 : 09 : 00
To Anne Reckett for the Child	01 : 00 : 00
To Gainsburgh for Thomas Peel	00 : 10 : 00
To R.R. which he disbursed	00 : 04 : 06
To be sent to the Quarterly Meeting	01 : 18 : 03

[1] 14th January, 1680. [2] 11th February, 1680.

This day Joseph Richardson of Brigg came into this Meeting and published his intentions of marriage with Anne Newbold of Hansworth Woodhouse in the County of Yorke, and brought a certificate from Balby monthly meeting, Certifying that they both there present had published their purpose of marrage there. Subscribed by her father and seaven other Friends.

This Monthly Meeting also sent their certificate to Balby meeting signifying the publication thereof here.

William Brown of Brigge and Rachel Easton of the same came also this day into the Meeting and there published their intentions of marriage each with other, and being the first tyme they are desired by Friends to wait till the next Monthly Meeting, where they are ordered to be present, to receive Friends answere.

The next meeting to be at Brigge.

Signed R. Rockhill.

p. 90.

At a Monthly Meeting held at the house of Thomas Markham in Glamfordbridge the third day of the first month 1679/80[1] :—

This day Joseph Richardson came the 2d tyme into this Meeting, signifying the continuance of his purpose of marriage with Anne Newbold, and all things being found clear on Josephs part (after signification of the like on the woemans part from Balby Monthly Meeting) they are left to the consumation thereof at their own conveniency, according to the good order of Truth.

William Brown & Rachel Easton both of Brigg came the second time into this Meeting, signifying their purpose of marriage, and Friends finding all things clear, left them to their liberty to accomplish the same at their conveniency according to the good order of Truth.

Humphrey Codd of Binbrooke & Joan Benington of Thealby came into this Meeting and declared their intentions of marriage each with other and being the first time, they are desired by Friends to wait till the next Monthly Meeting, where they are to be present to receive the answere of Friends.

John Benington of Thealeby, and Jane Johnson of Burton appeared also in this Meeting and published their intentions of marriage, and being the first tyme they are desired to wait till the next Monthly Meeting, where they are desired to be present, to receive Friends answere.

The next meeting ordered at Brigge.

Signed R. Rockhill.

[1] 3rd March, 1680.

At a Monthly Meeting held at the house of Thomas Markham in Glamfordbridge the fourteenth day 2d month 1680[1] :—

Ordered that Mary the daughter of George Hallywell deceased, be bound apprentice with William Nash of Scarburgh in the East Riding of Yorkshire, untill shee attaine the age of nineteen yeares, she was born the 2d day of the 10th month 1668[2] her master & dame are to find and provide for her all necessaries whatsoever dureing her whole terme.

Humphrey Codd of Binbrook & Joan Bennington of Thealby came this day the second tyme into this Meeting declaring the continuance of their purpose of marriage, and Friends finding all things clear, left them to their liberty to accomplish the same, at their own conveniency, according to the good order of Truth.

John Bennington of Thealby and Jane Johnson of Burton super Statther came the second tyme into this Meeting & signified the continuance of their purpose of marriage, and all things being found clear, Friends left them to their liberty to accomplish the same according to the Truth.

Richard Darkin of Gedney in the county of Lincolne, and Anne Hobson of Ealand in the Isle of Axholme, came into this Meeting and published their intentions of marriage each with other, which being the first tyme, they are desired to wait till the next Monthly Meeting, where they are ordered to be present.

Ordered that the next Meeting be at the house of John Wresle in Thealby.

Signed Robert Rockhill.

p. 91.

At a Monthly Meeting held at the house of John Wresle in Thealby the 12th day of the 3d month 1680[3] :—

George Nicholson of Burton Statther, for several disorders by him comitted, was censured by a Monthly Meeting of Friends held at Brigge the 14th of the 6th month 1678,[4] as by the record may appear, and Friends, for the space of 12 months after, having observed George to be very backward in submitting himselfe, & returning to the unity of Friends in the Truth, but forward enough in matters unwarrantable for him, as the case now standeth, did (in the feeling of true brotherly compassion) write to him from their Monthly Meeting at Boterwick the 10th day 7th month 1679[5] as by the record will also appear, & enclosed in their letter a copy of the aforesd censure as himselfe had desired. And this day this meeting received a writing from him thus truly transcribed.

[1] 14th April, 1680.
[2] 2nd December, 1668.
[3] 12th May, 1680.
[4] 14th August, 1678.
[5] 10th September, 1679.

Friends/ I received a paper from a Monthly Meeting held at Boterwick the 10th of the 7th month 79,[1] with another inclosed bearing no date, in both which I find diverse untruths inserted, wherefore I desire that you will give me another meeting, in order that there may be a right understanding betwixt us, the perticulars I shall not mention here because I judge it more proper when we are together, that objections may be answered on both sides. I desire no favour but equall Justice which is our Christian priviledge so I desire after serious consideration that you will return your answere. In the meantyme I rest, & am your friend, George Nicholson, dated the 12th of the 3d month 1680.[2] Whereto this meeting returned their answere by the mouth of a Friend, to this effect, That they had received his letter, & therein observed the stubbornness of his heart, and his continued reflections, and doe judge it his duty either to submitt to the aforesaid judgment, acknowledge his offences, & reconcile himselfe unto God, and to his brethren, or else appeale to the judgement of the Quarterly Meeting. (*Marginal Note:* Friends had a right understanding when they judged his case, and need not defend it with untruths, as here it is perversely suggested).

This day Richard Darkin of Gedney, & Anne Hobson of Eland came into this Meeting the second tyme, declaring the continuance of their purpose of marriage, & to receive Friends answere; who finding all things clear on the behalfe of both partyes, have approved thereof, and left the consummation to their own conveniency, according to the good order of Truth.

Ordered that a contribution be collected in the severall meetings belonging to this Monthly Meeting, & brought in to the next Monthly Meeting, from whence the necessityes of Friends being supplyed, remaindr sent to the Quarterly Meeting.

Ordered that the next Monthly Meeting be held at Gainsburgh.

Signed R. Rockhill.

At a Monthly Meeting held at the house of Henry Sympson in Gainsburgh the ninth day of the fourth month 1680[3]:—

		£	s.	d.	
Contributions	Gainsburgh	00	12	08	
	Garthorpe	00	12	01	
	Crowle	00	19	04	
	Wintringham ..	00	19	06	
	Brigge	00	17	04	
	Old stock sent in ..	00	07	01	04 : 08 : 00

[1] 10th September, 1679. [2] 12th May, 1680. [3] 9th June, 1680.

	£	s.	d.
To Anne Reckett for the Childe ..	02	00	00
Returnd back To Gainsburgh Meeting	00	12	00
To Crowle Meeting	00	09	06
	03	01	06
To be sent up to the Quarterly Meeting	01	06	06

The next Meeting ordered to be held at Robert Reeders house in Garthorpe.

Signed Robert Rockhill.

p. 92.

At a Monthly Meeting held at the house of Robert Reeder in Garthorpe the fourteenth day of the fifth month 1680[1] :—

Ordered that Thomas Wresle of Boterwick & William Snowdall of Ealand make enquirye of the estate of the families of James Dixon, Francis Brown and Robert Berryer, and if they stand in need of supply to give each of them five shillings for which the meeting will see them satisfyed, these 3 Friends with Robert Ashton were comitted to prison without bayle by Justice Darell only for refusing to pay the parish Clarke his demanded wages.

This day William Margrave of Garthorpe & Elizabeth Vessey of Belton came into this Meeting, and signified their purpose of marriage each with other, & being the first tyme, they are desired to waite for Friends answere till the next Monthly Meeting.

Ordered that the extraordinary contribution be forthwith collected and brought in to the next Monthly Meeting, which is to be held at Robt Ashton's house in Ealand.

Signed Robert Rockhill

At a Monthly Meeting held at the house of Robert Ashton in Ealand the eleventh day of the sixth month 1680[2] :—

		£	s.	d.
	Gainsburgh Meeting	00	10	08
Extraordinary contribution came in as followeth	Garthorpe	00	11	01–ob
	Crowle Meeting ..	00	15	08
	Wintringham ..	00	16	00
	Brigge	00	14	00
	totall –	03	07	05–ob

[1] 14th July, 1680. [2] 11th August, 1680.

This day William Margrave of Garthorpe, & Elizabeth Vessey of Belton came into this Meeting the second tyme & signifyed the continuance of their purpose of marriage, and this Meeting finding all things clear hath approved thereof, and left the consummation to their own conveniency, according to the good order of Truth.

Ordered that a contribution be collected in all the respective Perticuler Meetings and brought in to the next Monthly Meeting whence the wants of Friends being supplyed, the remainder to be sent up to the Quarterly Meeting.

The next Monthly Meeting ordered to be att Thomas Wresles house in Boterwick.

Signed R. Rockhill.

p. 93.

At a Monthly Meeting held at the house of Thomas Wresle in Boterwick the eighth day of the seaventh month 1680[1] :—

		£	s.	d.
Contributions came in as followeth	Gainsburgh ..	00	12	09
	Crowle ..	00	18	00
	Garthorp ..	00	11	06
	Wintringham	00	15	03
	Brigge ..	00	15	00
	totall	03	12	00
Returnd back for the supply of poor Friends	To Crowle ..	01	07	06
	To Gainsburgh	0	15	00
	totall	02	02	06
To be sent up to the Quarterly Meeting		01	10	00

According to former order Thomas Wresle disbursed twelve shillings six pence to the supply of the families of Francis Brown, James Dixon and Robert Berrier being prisoners at that tyme on Truths account whereof this Meeting hath now reimbursed him.

The next meeting to be at Brigge.

Signed Robert Rockhill.

At a Monthly Meeting held at the house of Thomas Markham in Glamford Bridge the 13th day of October 1680 :—

The great inconvenience of continuing the weekly Meeting att Wootton being laid before this Meeting, they doe in brotherly love (for the advantage of such Friends as cannot goe up to

[1] 8th September, 1680.

Wootton when the Meeting falls to be there, and forasmuch as the reason of its being kept there, is ceased advise & councill Robert Richardson to dispense[1] with the removall of the Meeting from his house at least for the winter season ; the furtherance of the Truth being the chief thing we all should intend.

This Meeting being acquainted with the proceedings of the Quarterly Meeting concerning George Nicholson, doe think it necessary that G. Nicholson appear at the next Monthly Meeting for the better satisfaction of Friends thereunto belonging, and that he may be received into the fellowship of Friends in unity of the Truth, and Anthony Shankster & John Benington are ordered to acquaint him with it.

This day Thomas Haslehurst of Stockwith and Dorcas Johnson of Burton Statther came into this Meeting, and declared their purpose of marriage, And being the first tyme, they are desired to wait till the next Monthly Meeting, where they both are ordered to be present to receive the answer of Friends.

The next Monthly Meeting ordred to be at Boterwick.

Signed Robert Rockhill.

p. 94.

At a Monthly Meeting held at the house of Thomas Wresle in Boterwick the tenth day of November 1680 :—

This day according to former order, George Nicholson came before this Meeting and did there freely & fully own that writing which was drawn up at the last Quarterly Meeting at Lincolne, as his voluntary act & deed, and not extorted by any force, or over-ruling persuasions with which acknowledgment Friends of this meeting are at present satifyed. The writing is recorded as followeth :—

I George Nicholson, being one who have been long convinced of the Lord's Truth amongst you, whereby I have witnessed in days past, a growth & good degree of increase in the same, to my true joy. But, alas, alas, since that, for want of faithfulness unto him that called me out of darknes ; the enemies of my soul hath greatly prevailed against me & brought a thick cloud over my understanding, and led me into a wrong spirit, in & by which (to the hurt of my own soul) I have been led into prejudice against diverse of the Lord's people belonging to the Monthly Meeting of Gainsburgh ; & in that spirit have spoken & written very unsavorylie & foolishly, to the grieving of the good spirit of God, in my own perticular, & also of the Church of God more in generall. Wherefore I am grieved that I should be thus led aside to offend diverse of the Lords servants, who have tyme after tyme sought to reclaim me. Therefore, of all such whome I have wronged by word or deed,

[1] *i.e.*, put up with.

I do intreat forgiveness of my trespasses against them, as they desire the Lord may forgive them ; hoping that for the future I shall so keep my watch to the Lord, as I may be preserved by his holy power so as for time to come to walk wisely, and give no occasion neither to Jew nor Gentile, nor unto the Church of God. Written the 29th day of the seaventh month,[1] for the clearing of the blessed Truth, & for the satisfaction of all concerned. And if the Lord please to open my understanding more largely in this matter, I hope to answere the Lords requiring, to the satisfaction of all.

Wittnes my hand George Nicholson.

Witneses hereunto. John Theaker, William Dixon, Thomas Robinson, Thomas Sowter, Thomas Summers, Stephen Willowby.

George Nicholson desired the Meeting might be again restored to his house (which had been removed thence for the cause of his offences) the Meeting hath taken notice of it & will determine it in tyme convenient.

Ordered that a contribution be forthwith collected in all the Particular Meetings belonging to this Monthly Meeting, and brought in to the next Monthly Meeting, from whence the necessityes of Friends being supplyed, the remainder to be sent up to the Quarterly Meeting.

Order — This day Thomas Haslehurst and Dorcas Johnson came the second tyme into this Meeting, signifying the continuance of their purpose of marriage & to receive Friends answere, who having nothing against it have left the consumation thereof to their own conveniency according to the good order of Truth.

The next Meeting ordered to be at Brigge.

Signed Robert Rockhill.

p. 95.

At a Monthly Meeting held at the house of Thomas Markham in Glamfordbridge the 8 day of the tenth month 1680[2] :—

		£	s.	d.
Contributions came in as followeth	Gainsburgh ..	00	11	10
	Crowle ..	00	16	00
	Wintringham	00	17	00
	Brigge ..	00	19	06
	Old stock added		04	03
	Totall	03	08	07
	Garthorp ..	00	09	00

[1] 29th September. [2] 8th December, 1680.

		£	s.	d.
Returned :	To Vincent Brownlow for John Halliwell	01 :	00 :	00
	To Joseph Richardson for N.W. his coate	01 :	00 :	01
	To Gainsburgh for supply of their poor	01 :	08 :	06

George Nicholsons motion of having the Meeting restored to his house, was this day considered, but Wintringham Friends alleadging the inconveniency thereof for severall reasons, the finall determination thereof is referred to the next Monthly Meeting, which is appointed to be at Brigge.

Signed Robert Rockhill.

At a Monthly Meeting held at the house of Thomas Markham in Brigge the 12th day of the eleventh month 1680[1] :—

According to the abovesaid referrence, the busines of George Nicholson was considered and for diverse good reasons alleadged by Friends of Wintringham Meeting it is ordered and concluded by this Meeting, that the weekly Meeting aforesaid be not resettled at Burton Statther, that being the utmost corner, but kept two dayes at Wintringham & two dayes at Thealby, for the ease of that corner.

Whereas formerly when Friends were endeavouring to reconcile the difference between George Nicholson & Joseph Pope, George Nicholson sent severall letters to one William David (who was not a Friend) therein much reflecting upon, & complaining against severall Freinds as unwise, & unjust, who not understanding his case (as he suggested) yet would adventure to give away his right. Since which tyme George Nicholson hath submitted himselfe to the Judgment of Friends & owned his condemnation (as by the left hand page appeareth). It is therefore ordered by Friends in this Monthly Meeting assembled that Thomas Wresle & Anthony Westoby, acquaint George Nicholson that it is the mind of this Meeting, and Friends doe admonish him, by writing to take off those aspersions & scandalls from Friends which his inconsiderate pen hath laid upon them, and send or bring his writing first unto the Monthly Meeting that Friends may consider it, & they are to bring an account of his answere to the next Monthly Meeting.

Ordered that a contribution be forthwith collected, in the Perticuler Meetings respectively and brought in to the next Monthly Meeting, whence the necessityes of poor Friends being supplyed, the rest to be sent up to the Quarterly Meeting. The next Meeting ordered to be at Brigge.

Signed Robert Rockhill.

[1] 12th January, 1681.

p. 96.

At a Monthly Meeting held at the house of Thomas Markham in Glamfordbridge the ninth day of the twelth month 1680[1] :—

Thomas Wresle & Anthony Westoby according to former order, recount unto this Meeting the answere of George Nicholson, which not being satisfactory, the same persons are ordered to speak to George the second tyme, and bring an account of his answere to the next Monthly Meeting.

		£	s.	d.
	Gainsburgh ..	00	18	10
Contribucions came	Crowle ..	01	00	01
in as followeth	Brigge ..	01	09	00
	Garthorpe ..	00	16	10
	Wintringham	01	09	06
	totall	05	14	03
Sent back for supply				
of poor Friends	to Gainsburgh	01	02	06
	Anne Reckett	02	00	00
	Wintringham	00	08	06
	Garthorp ..	00	13	00
	Crowle ..	00	02	00
	Brigge ..	00	02	06
Remaines	Remaines 01 : 05 : 09	04	08	06

The next Meeting appointed to be at Boterwick.

Signed Robert Rockhill.

Att a Monthly Meeting held at the house of Thomas Wresle in Boterwick the 9th day of the first month 1680/1[2] :—

This day Thomas Foster of Crowle & Anna Spencer of Thorne appeared in this Meeting signifying their intentions of marriage the father of the said Anna was also present & testified his consent.

Also David Chessman and Avis Wells both of Belton signified their purpose of marriage to this meeting which being the first tyme the Meeting hath taken both into consideration & ordered the partyes to be present at the next Monthly Meeting which is appointed to be at Eland.

Signed Robert Rockhill.

[1] 9th February, 1681. [2] 9th March, 1681.

p 97.

Att a Monthly Meeting held at the house of Robert Ashton in Eland the 13th day of the second month 1681[1] :—

Thomas Wresle and Anthony Westaby recount unto this Meeting the answere of George Nicholson, which is that he can give no other answere than what he gave before, which Friends of this meeting judged unsatisfactory.

This day Thomas Foster of Crowle and Hannah Spencer of Thorn in the County of Yorke came into this Meeting the 2d tyme signifying the continuance of their purpose of marriage, and brought a certificate from Balby Monthly Meeting testifying their approbation, and consent of parents, now this Meeting finding all things clear have also approved thereof, and left the consummation to their own conveniency according to the good order of Truth.

David Chessman and Ave Wels both of Belton came also the 2d tyme into this Meeting & signifyed the continuance of their purpose of marriage & Friends having nothing against it, have approved thereof & left the consummation to their own conveniency, according to the good order of Truth

The next Monthly Meeting ordered to be at Thealby.

Signed R. Rockhill.

At a Monthly Meeting held at the house of John Wresle of Thealby the eleventh day of the third month 1681[2] :—

Forasmuch as George Nicholson hath severall tymes refused to give unto Freinds of this meeting just satisfaction, in taking off such accusations, reflections & aspersions as he had formerly laid upon severall Friends in a letter by him written & sent unto William Davie, though severall tymes thereto admonished; It is ordered by this Meeting that Robert Rockhill transcribe the writing of George Nicholson his submission, and subscribe it on the behalfe of this meeting, & send it to William Davie by the hand of John Clarke of Garthorp for the justifying of Friends concerned, & for the clearing of the Truth.

This day John Potter of Lea-wood and Anne Reckett of Gate Burton appeared in this Meeting & signified their purpose of marriage each with other, which being the first tyme, they are desired to wait till the next Monthly Meeting where they are ordered to be present, to receive Friends answere.

Ordered that a contribution be collected throughout all the Meetings and brought in to the next Monthly Meeting, whence Friends

[1] 13th April, 1681. [2] 11th May, 1681.

necessityes being supplyed, the remainder to be brought in to the Quarterly Meeting.

The next Monthly Meeting ordered to be at Gainsburgh.

Signed Robert Rockhill.

p. 98.

Att a Monthly Meeting of Friends held at Gainsburgh the eighth day of the fourth moneth 1681[1] :—

		£	s.	d.	
Contributions came in as followeth	Crowle ..	00	18	00	ob
	Wintringham	01	00	09	
	Garthorpe ..	00	12	00	
	Gainsburgh ..	00	10	10	
	Brigge ..	00	14	00	
	old stock ..	00	02	09	
		03	18	04	ob

	£	s.	d.	
Returned for the supply of Brigg poor	00	14	00	
to Anne Reckett last payment for Mary Codd	01	10	00	
for the supply of Crowle poor	00	10	00	
to be sent up to the Quarterly Meeting ..	01	04	04	ob
	03	18	04	ob

This day John Potter of Lea-wood & Anne Reckett of Gateburton appeared in this Meeting the second time signifying the continuance of their purpose of marriage and expecting the answere of Friends who finding all things clear, and no just impediment have pronounced their approbation thereof, and left the consummation to their own conveniency, according to the good order of Truth.

The next Monthly Meeting ordered to be at Adlinfleete. The eighth day of the 4th moneth 1681.[1]

Signed R. Rockhill.

Received of Friends of the Monthly Meeting of Gainsburgh the summe of thirty shillings being the last payment & in full of seaven pounds and ten shillings which was due unto me from this meeting for the keeping of Mary, one of the daughters of Christopher Codd late deceased untill shee be aged eighteen years, according to a certain agreement made between me the said Anne Reckett and Friends of the Monthly Meeting bearing date the eighth day of the seaventh moneth 1679.[2] I say received in full thirty shillings, by me Anne Reckett her marke.

[1] 8th June, 1681. [2] 8th September, 1679.

At a Monthly Meeting held at Adlinfleet the thirteenth day of the fifth moneth 1681[1] :—

Whereas complaint hath been made unto this Meeting that Edward Chessman of Belton did fell and cutt down severall young trees in a certain close in Beltoft which he farmed only for one year, which matter of fact Edward himselfe hath confessed, It is therefore the Judgment of this Meeting that Edward Chessman hath done wrong in so doing, to the dammage of the owner of the said Close and Friends doe admonish him to make ample satisfaction for the same and that with all convenient speed, and also to give his partner the one moiety of 3*s.* which was deposited in his hand for satisfaction of some trespasses done to himselfe and partner at the farming of another close.

Whereas some Friends have moved for the discontinuance of the Meeting at Edward Chessmans house, by reason of the many scandalls and reproaches that are cast upon the Truth and Friends by his (*p. 99.*) miscarriages; Friends of this meeting doe referre the determination of that busines to the judgment & discresion of the Isle Meeting who are most concernd therein, so as they endeavour to doe all things for the Glory of God, and the advancement of his blessed Truth.

Complaint being made to this Meeting, that John Hallywell (whom Friends putt apprentice with Vincent Brownlow) is departed from his master. It is ordered that Robert Rockhill & Joseph Richardson desire Vincent Brownlow to be present at the next Monthly Meeting to give an account of his said apprentice.

The next Meeting ordered to be at Boterwick.

Signed Robert Rockhill.

At a Monthly Meeting of Friends held at Boterwick the tenth day of the sixth month 1681[2] :—

This day Vincent Brownlow came into this Meeting according to former order and did satisfy Friends that his apprentice John Halliwell had not any just cause to depart from his service, and that since his departure he hath severall tymes made enquirie after him but cannot (as yet) heare of him, so that Friends of this meeting have not anything to charge Vincent Brownlow withall concerning his said apprentice, yet in regard he was a Friends child, Friends of this meeting doe purpose to take some other course to find him.

Ordered that a contribution be collected throughout all the Perticuler Meetings and brought in to the next Monthly Meeting, whence

[1] 13th July, 1681. [2] 10th August, 1681.

Friends necessityes being supplyed, the remainder to be sent up to the Quarterly Meeting.

The next Monthly Meeting appointed at the house of John Pilsworth in Belton.

Signed Robert Rockhill.

At a Monthly Meeting of Friends held at the house of John Pilsworth in Belton the fourteenth day of September 1681 :—

Ordered that Robert Rockhill write notes to the severall Monthly Meetings belonging to this Quarterly Meeting, to make enquirie throughout their Particuler Meetings after John Halliwell, that if possible he may not be lost.

				s. d.
Contributions came in as followeth	Crowle meeting	00 : 17 : 01	sent to Crowl	3 6
	Gainsburgh ..	00 : 10 : 00		
	Garthorpe ..	00 : 11 : 10		
	Wintringham	00 : 15 : 06		
	Brigge ..	00 : 00 : 00		
Sent up to the Quarterly Meeting		03 : 00 : 00		

This day Vincent Brownlow came into this Meeting, signifying his purpose to joyne in marriage with Mary Huntington of Kingston upon Hull, and brought a certifycate from the Monthly Meeting in Holdernes signifying both their personall appearance their concerning the same thing, and their approbation thereof, desireing a certificate from this Monthly Meeting, which R. Rockhill is ordered to draw up and send accordingly.

Next Monthly Meeting ordered to be at Brigge.

Signed R. Rockhill.

p. 100.

At a Monthly Meeting of Friends held at the house of Thomas Markham in Glamfordbriggs the 12th day of October 1681 :—

This day Vincent Brownlow came into this Meeting the 2d tyme & brought another certificate from the Monthly Meeting in Holdernes, signifying his 2d appearance in person there, & hers by certificate, intimating the continuance of their purpose of marriage, and Friends of Holdernes Monthly Meeting their approbation of the same, now, noe impediment appearing to obstruct their proceeding, they are left by this meeting to their own conveniency in the consummation of their said purpose, according to the good order of Truth.

This day Matthew Jackson of Gainsburgh & Hannah Thurgate of the same came into this Meeting and signified their purpose to take each other in marriage, and being the first tyme of publication, they are desired to wait till the next Monthly

Meeting, where they are to be present to receive the answere of Friends.

The next meeting to be at Boterwick.

Signed R. Rockhill.

At a Monthly Meeting held at Boterwick in Thomas Wresles house the ninth day of November 1681 :—

This day Matthew Jackson of Gainesburgh and Hannah Thurgate of the same, came into this Meeting the second tyme & signifyed the continuance of their purpose to take each other in marriage and Friends finding all things clear on both parts have given their consents to the same, leaving the consummation thereof to their own conveniency, according to the good order of Truth.

Ordered that fifteen shillings be sent from this Meeting unto Edmond Morley for the supply of two poor widdowes, to wit, eight shillings for Tomisson Tranmore & 7*s*. for widdow Pickhaver, sent by Thomas Pepper of Ustfleet.

Ordered that a contribution be collected and brought in to the next Monthly Meeting, whence the wants of poor Friends being supplyed, the remainder to be carryed up to the Quarterly Meeting.

The next Monthly Meeting ordered to be at Brigge.

Signed R. Rockhill.

At a Monthly Meeting at Thomas Markhams 10br the 19th 1681[1] :—

		£	s.	d.	
Contributions came in	Gainsburgh	00	10	03	
	Crowle ..	00	17	10	sent back to Crowle for the funerall of Symon Rosse & supply of other poor Friends by R. Ashton 01 : 03 : 06
	Wintringham	01	00	00	
	Brigge ..	00	16	06	
	Garthorpe ..				

To be sent up to the Quarterly Meeting .. .. 02 : 01 : 00

The next Meeting ordered to be at Brigge.

Signed Robert Rockhill.

p. 101.

At a Monthly Meeting of Friends held at the house of Thomas Markham in Glamfordbridge the 11th day of the 11th month 1681[2] :

This day William Smith of Elsham and Joan Richardson of Brigge came into this Meeting and declared their purpose to take

[1] 19th December, 1681. [2] 11th January, 1682.

each other in marriage and being the first tyme they are desired to wait the answere of Friends till the next Monthly Meeting where they are desired to be present.

Also William Prigion of North Hykham in the county of Lincolne and Mary Northen of Torksey came into this Meeting signifying their purpose of marriage each with other & being the first tyme they are desired to wait till the next Monthly Meeting where they are to be present.

The next Meeting appointed to be att Brigge.

Signed Robert Rockhill.

At a Monthly Meeting held at the house of Thomas Markham in Glamford Bridge the eighth day of the twelth month 1681[1] :—

This day William Smith of Elsham and Joan Richardson of Brigge came into this Meeting the 2d tyme signifying their continuance in their purpose of marriage each with other, and Friends finding all things clear on behalf of both parties declared their unity with, and approbation of the same and left the consummation thereof to their own conveniency according to the Truth.

Ordered that a contribution be collected and brought in to the next Monthly Meeting whence the wants of Friends being supplyed the remainder to be carryed up to the Quarterly Meeting.

The next Monthly Meeting appointed to be att West Boterwick.

Signed R. Rockhill.

At a Monthly Meeting of Friends held at Boterwick 8 day 1st month 1681/2[2] :—

	£ s. d.		£ s. d.
Contributions came in		sent back	
Gainsburgh ..	0 : 12 : 4	by Peter Naylor	0 : 7 : 0
Crowle ..	0 : 19 : 0	by Robert Ashton	0 : 7 : 8
Wintringham ..	0 : 18 : 6	by Robert Vessey	0 : 18 : 8
Garthrop ..	0 : 11 : 0	Thomas Nainby	0 : 2 : 0
Brigge ..	0 : 16 : 0		
Old Stock ..	0 : 8 : 6		
			1 : 15 : 4
	4 : 5 : 4	To be sent to Quarterly Meeting	2 : 10 : 0

This day William Prigion of North Hikham came the 2d tyme into this Meeting declaring his purpose to joyn in marriage with Mary Northing, and brought a certificate under her hand

[1] 8th February, 1682. [2] 8th March, 1682.

signifying her consent so all things being clear on both sides, the consummation thereof is left to their own conveniency according to the good order of Truth.

Anne Spain of Garthorpe having sent a complaint to this Meeting that there are certaine reckonings betwixt her and Joseph Pope which shee desires may be ended. This Meeting therefore orders Thomas Wresle of Wintringham and George Nicholson to desire Joseph Pope to come to the next Monthly Meeting, and there show cause why he delays to accompt with her.

The next Monthly Meeting appointed to be at Thealby.

Signed Robert Rockhill.

p. 102.

Att a Monthly Meeting held at the house of John Wresle of Thealby the twelth day of the second month 1682[1] :—

This day Joseph Pope came into this Meeting, expressing his willingness to end the difference betwixt him and Anne Spain, whereupon this Meeting referred the hearing & determination thereof unto Robert Scott, Robert Langley, Thomas Markham and Edmond Morley, or any three of them and ordered Joseph Pope to give such seasonable notice to the said parties as the difference may be finally composed before the next Monthly Meeting, and then an account to be given thereof.

This day Thomas Barrow of Haxey and Hester Lawrence of Beltoft came into this Meeting and signified their purpose of marriage each with other, and being but the first tyme they are to wait the answer of the next Monthly Meeting, where they are to be present.

The next Monthly Meeting appointed at the house of Henry Sympson in Gainsburgh. Signed Robert Rockhill.

Att a Monthly Meeting held at the house of Henry Sympson in Gainsburgh the 10th day of the 3d moneth 1682[2] :—

There being no account given to this Meeting of the agreement between Joseph Pope and Anne Spain, according to the appointment of the last Monethly Meeting ; it is this day ordered that Robert Collyer & Robert Rockhill give notice thereof to some Friends of Wintringham Meeting, that they may speak to Joseph Pope to use all diligence in the dispatch of that business (if it be not already done) and give an account thereof to the next Monthly Meeting.

This day Thomas Barrow and Hester Lawrence came the second tyme into this Meeting, and signifyed the continuance of

[1] 12th April, 1682. [2] 10th May, 1682.

their purpose of marriage, and Friends finding all things clear on both sides have given their approbation, leaving the consummation thereof to their own conveniency according to the good order of Truth.

Ordered that a contribution be collected in the severall Meetings and brought in to the next Monthly Meeting, whence the necessityes of Friends being supplyed, the rest to be sent to the Quarterly Meeting.

The next Monthly Meeting appointed at the house of Christopher Wilson in Adlinfleet.

Signed Robert Rockhill.

At a Monthly Meeting held at the house of Christopher Willson in Adlinfleet the 14th day of the 4th month 1682[1] :—

This Meeting being informed that the difference between Joseph Pope & Anne Spain is not yet determined and for the more speedy dispatch thereof (it having already too long depended) it is determined and concluded by this Meeting that Thomas Markham, Edmond Morley, Thomas Wresle of Boterwick and R. Rockhill doe meet together upon the 5th day of the 5th month next at the house of Robert Reeder in Garthorp, then and there finally to determine the busines and such other understanding Friends as can be gotten together are to be also present.

Contributions came in as followeth.

p. 103.

Gainsburgh ..	00 : 12 : 03		
Crowle ..	00 : 18 : 04	returned back to Crowle	00 : 19 : 00
Wintringham ..	01 : 02 : 00		
Garthorpe ..	00 : 13 : 04	to Garthorpe	00 : 03 : 5
Brigg	00 : 16 : 06		
			01 : 02 : 05
	04 : 02 : 05		
		To be sent up to the Quarterly Meeting ..	03 : 00 : 00

Ordred that Robert Ashton, Thomas Wresle of Boterwick and Francis Brown take care about the repairing of the house that was George Hallywells, wherein Widdow Chapman and Widdow Moseley now dwell, and give an accompt of the charge to this meeting, who will see them indempnifyed.

The next meeting to be at Robert Ashtons house in Ealand.

Signed Robert Rockhill.

[1] 14th June, 1682.

At a Monthly Meeting held at the house of Robert Ashton in Ealand the twelth day of the fifth month 1682[1] :—

Forasmuch as the difference between Joseph Pope and Anne Spain hath been lately heard and determined, but not to the full satisfaction of all the parties engaged in that service ; it is concluded by this Meeting that Thomas Markham and John Hogge procure a meeting with Anthony Wels of Hull, with all possible speed, to review the accounts and putt a finall end to that difference, in whose award this Meeting and the partyes more particularly concerned will acquiesce.

The next meeting appointed at the house of Thomas Wresle in Boterwick.

Signed Robert Rockhill.

At a Monthly Meeting held at the house of Thomas Wresle in Boterwick the 9th day of the 6 month 1682[2] :—

Ordered that a contribution be collected throughout all the Meetings belonging to this Monthly Meeting, and brought up to the next Monthly Meeting whence the wants of Friends being supplyed, the remainder to be sent up to the Quarterly Meeting.

Ordered that Thomas Markham be desired to make speedy despatch with Anthony Wells and John Hogge, of Joseph Popes and Anne Spaines business before the next Monthly Meeting which is to be at Thomas Markhams house in Brigge.

Signed Robert Rockhill.

p. 104.

Att a Monthly Meeting held at the house of Thomas Markham in Brigge the 13 day of September 1682 :—

According to the order of the Monthly Meeting held at Ealand the 12th day of the 5th month 1682[3], Thomas Markham and John Hogge have conferred & advised with Anthony Wells of Hull about the accompts between Joseph Pope and Anne Spain, as adjusted by John Hogge after the stateing of them by the parties appointed by the Monthly Meeting held at Christopher Wilsons house in Adlinfleet the 14th day of the 4th[4] month last past, and the said accompts by Anthony Wells are declared to be right wherein Anne Spain is found debtor to Joseph Pope and with this the Meeting is satisfyed and the parties concerned have promised to acquiesce.

[1] 12th July, 1682. [2] 9th August, 1682. [3] 12th July, 1682.
[4] 14th June, 1682.

Contributions came in	Gainsburgh	00 : 11 : 04
	Garthorpe	00 : 14 : 04
	Crowle	00 : 17 : 09
	Wintringham	01 : 00 : 00
	Brigg	00 : 15 : 00
	Stock	01 : 03 : 11
		05 : 02 : 04
Returned by Matthew Jackson		0 : 1 : 2
by John Pilsworth		0 : 5 : 0
by Robert Vessey		0 : 5 : 0
		0 : 11 : 2
To be sent to the Quarterly Meeting		02 : 10 : 00
Stock in Thomas Markhams hands		02 : 01 : 2

This day Thomas Nainby of Glamfordbridge came into this Meeting and declared his purpose of marriage with Isabel Killingar of Gillfitt in the county of Yorke, and brought a certificate from their meeting at Hakethorpe, that he had declared the same there which being the first tyme of publication here, we have given him our certificate, and refferred him to our next Monthly Meeting which is to be at Boterwick.

Signed R. Rockhill.

At a Monthly Meeting held at the house of Thomas Wresle in Boterwick the 11th day of the 8th month 1682[1] :—

Ordered that Henry Sympson for Gainsburgh, Thomas Wresle for Crowle, Robert Reeder for Garthorp, Thomas Wresle for Wintringham & Thomas Markham for Brigg (according to the mind of the last Quarterly Meeting) doe take the subscriptions of such persons as are able & willing to contribute to the great suffrings of Robert Hopkinson and others and what moneys shall be soe subscribed to receive the same and bring it up to the next Quarterly Meeting.

This day Thomas Nainby came into this meeting the 2d time, signifying the continuance of his purpose to take Isabell Killingar to wife, and brought another certificate from the Monthly Meeting to which she belongs *(p. 105.)* signifying her willingnes, and clearnes from any impediment which may hinder their said purpose ; so Friends of this Meeting being satisfyed that all things are clear on his part, have approved of their purpose, and left the consummation thereof to their own conveniency, according to the good order of Truth.

[1] 11th October, 1682.

Ordered that two contributions be collected and brought to the Monthly Meeting next before the next Quarterly Meeting whence the wants of Friends being supplyed, the rest to be sent up to the Quarterly Meeting.

The next Monthly Meeting ordered to be at Brigge.

Signed Robert Rockhill.

At a Monthly Meeting of Friends held at the house of Thomas Markham in Brigge the eighth day of November 1682 :—

Ordered by this Meeting that some of the Isle Friends lay down five shillings for payment of Jane Carnells rent, and deduct it out of the next contribution and give accompt thereof to the next Monthly Meeting.

Ordered that Joseph Richardson give unto Helene Crowther five shillings, for supply of her wants, which is to be allowed him the next Monthly Meeting. Which is ordered to be att Brigge.

Signed Robert Rockhill.

At a Monthly Meeting held at the house of Thomas Markham in Glamfordbridge the 13th day of December 1682 :—

Ordered that William Harrison of Wintringham & Thomas Wrestle of the same, do bring in to the next Monthly Meeting the last will & inventory of the goods of James Tayler of Whitton late deceased, that they may be recorded in the book for that purpose provided.

Contributions came in :

Gainsburgh	..	00 : 18 : 00	
Crowle	..	01 : 00 : 00	returnd ——— 00 : 15 : 03 by Francis Brown
Wintringham	..	01 : 08 : 00	
Garthorp	..	00 : 16 : 06	
Brigge	..	01 : 00 : 00	——— by Joseph Richardson 00 – 05 – 00
old stock	..	01 : 00 : 00	
		05 : 02 : 03	the abovesaid sum deducted.

To be sent to the Quarterly Meeting ——05 : 00 : 00. Stock in Thomas Markham's hand ——— 01 : 02 : 03.

This day John Scott of Crowle declared his purpose of marriage with Dorothy Barlow of Leeds in the County of Yorke and brought a certificate of the publication thereof in that Monthly

Meeting as also of her parents consent which being the first time of publication here, he is desired to wait untill the next Monthly Meeting.

The next Meeting appointed to be att Brigge.

Signed Robert Rockhill.

p. 106.

At a Monthly Meeting held at the house of Thomas Markham in Glamfordbridge the 10th day of the 11th month 1682[1] :—

This day according to former order Thomas Wrestle of Wintringham brought in the last will and inventory of James Tayler of Whitton deceased, to be recorded in Friends book for that purpose provided.

This day John Scott of Crowle came the second time into this Meeting declaring the continuance of his purpose of marriage with Dorothy Barlow of Leeds in the County of Yorke, and Friends of this Meeting having nothing against it on his part have granted their certificate to the Monthly Meeting for them parts of their unitie therewith and referre the finall conclusion of that business to Friends of their own Monthly Meeting.

The next Monthly Meeting appointed to be att Brigge.

Signed Robert Rockhill.

At a Monthly Meeting of Friends held at the house of Thomas Markham in Glamfordbridge the 14th day of the 12th month 1682[2] :

It is ordered by this Meeting that a contribution be collected in each Perticuler Meeting, and brought into the next Monthly Meeting, whence the necessities of Friends being supplyed the rest to be sent up to the Quarterly Meeting, and if it so fall out that the Quarterly Meeting happen upon the day of oure Monthly Meeting, then Friends are desired to meet upon that account the fourth day before.

sent for supply of Friends per Edmond Morley..	01 : 05 : 00
to Brigg poor by T. Markham	00 : 10 : 00
	01 : 15 : 00
Stock in Thomas Markham hand ..	01 : 00 : 07

The next Monthly Meeting ordered at Thomas Wresles house in Boterwick.

Signed Robert Rockhill.

[1] 10th January, 1683. [2] 14th February, 1683.

Att a Monthly Meeting of Friends held at the house of Thomas Wresle of Boterwick the 14 of the 1st month 1682/3[1] :—

Complaint being made to this Meeting that the wife and children of James Dixon of Crowle are in want and need supply by reason of her husbands long imprisonment and deteiner from his employment. It is therefore desired by this Meeting that Robert Ashton take care for their necessary supply till the next Monthly Meeting, who will see him indempnified.

Contributions came in	Crowle	00 : 15 : 00
	Garthorpe	00 : 12 : 00
	Brigg	00 : 16 : 00
	Gainsburgh	00 : 11 : 00
	Wintringham	00 : 18 : 00
		03 : 12 : 00
sent back by Thomas Wrestle		0 : 5 : 8
by Robert Reeder		0 : 6 : 8
Sent to Quarterly Meeting		02 : 10 : 00
Stock in Thomas Markham hand		01 : 10 : 08

This day Edward Rockhill of Adlingfleet and Mary Richardson of Brigg came into this Meeting and declared their purpose of marriage each with other, which being the first time of publication they are desired to waite till the next Monthly Meeting where they are also to be present.

The next Meeting appointed at the house of John Wresle in Thealby.

Signed Robert Rockhill.

p. 107.

At a Monthly Meeting held at the house of John Wresle of Thealby the 11th day of the 2nd month 1683[2] :—

Ordered that a contribution for the reliefe of John Southwell of Sibsey & others who had his house and goods consumed with fire be forthwith collected and brought in to the next Monthly Meeting, and that notice hereof be sent in writing to each Perticuler Meeting.

This day Edward Rockhill of Adlingfleet came into this Meeting the second time and Mary Richardson by certificate under the hands of her father, her mother and her selfe, signifying their approbation and concent, and continuance of her purpose of marriage with the said Edward Rockhill, and Friends of

[1] 14th March, 1683. [2] 11th April, 1683.

this meeting finding all things fair and clear of both partyes and nothing appearing to hinder their proceedings, doe hereby declare their approbation of and unitie with the said marriage, and referre the consumation thereof to their own conveniency, according to the good order of Truth.

This day Henry Whiteside of Rawcliffe in the county of Yorke and Dorcas Haslehurst of Thealby in the county of Lincolne came into this Meeting and declared their purpose of marriage each with other, and being the first tyme, they are desired to wait till the next Monthly Meeting where they are to be present.

The next Meeting appointed att the house of Robert Reeder in Garthorp.

Signed Robert Rockhill.

At a Monthly Meeting held at the house of Robert Reeder in Garthorpe the 9 day of the third month 1683[1] :—

Contributions for John Southwell came in	Gainsburgh ..	00 : 11 : 01
	Crowle	00 : 15 : 00
	Winteringham ..	00 : 19 : 06
	Garthorpe ..	00 : 12 : 00
	Brigge	00 : 12 : 00
		03 : 09 : 07

This day Henry Whiteside and Dorcas Haslehurst came into this Meeting the 2nd tyme confirming their purpose of marriage, & brought a certificate from the Monthly Meeting at Warnesworth signifying their proceedings there, & the approbation of that Monthly Meeting, now Friends of this Meeting finding all things clear have also given their approbation, & referred the accomplishment to their own conveniency, according to the good order of Truth.

Ordered that a contribution be collected and brought in to the next Monthly Meeting whence the wants of Friends being supplied, the rest bring up to the Quarterly Meeting.

Ordered that the next Monthly Meeting be held at the house of Henry Simpson in Gainsburgh upon the second sixth day of the next month, being the 8th day thereof and so to continue for the future unless Friends of Gainsborough Meeting, give weighty reasons to the contrary.

Signed Robert Rockhill.

[1] 9th May, 1683.

p. 108.

At a Monthly Meeting held at the house of Henry Simpson in Gainsburgh the eighth day of the fourth month 1683[1] :—

Contributions as followeth				
	Gainsburgh ..	00 : 10 : 06	....	00 : 08 : 00
	Brigge ..	00 : 14 : 00		
	Garthorp ..	00 : 12 : 00	....	00 : 05 : 00
	Wintringham	00 : 18 : 03	sent back	
	Crowle ..	00 : 16 : 06	....	00 : 07 : 06
	old stock ..	01 : 09 : 03		
				01 : 00 : 06
		05 : 00 : 06	to the Quarterly Meeting ..	04 : 00 : 00

Ordered that enquiry be made whether Friends marriages be recorded at large with the names of the wittnesses present at the marriage and reported the next Monthly Meeting.

Upon complaint of Friends belonging to Garthorp Meeting that the holding of the Monthly Meetings upon the fourth day of the weeke is very inconvenient for them, as being the usual day of their chapmens access to buy their goods and fatt cattell so that they have been constrained to neglect either the one or the other, to the damage either of their own private concernes or publick service of the Truth. Therefore at their request it is ordered by this Meeting that from henceforth for the tyme to come, the Monthly Meetings be held at the severall places successively to be appointed, upon the second sixth day of each month respectively, and that the next Monthly Meeting be held at the house of Robert Ashton Ealand.

Signed Robert Rockhill.

At a Monthly Meeting held at the house of Robert Ashton in Ealand the thirteenth day of the fifth month 1683 in Ealand[2] :—

It is ordered by Friends of this Meeting that from henceforth all Friends who shall hereafter be joyned in marriage doe bring or send their certificates of marriage to Robert Rockhill to be by him recorded at large in the book for that purpose provided, that if any should happen to be (lost or otherwise destroyed) they may have the same renewed out of the record.

This day Dennis Marshall of Bilton in the county of Yorke, and Hannah Wake of Glamfordbrigg in the county of Lincolne appeared in this Meeting, the one by proxey (his indispensible occasions wherewith the meeting is satisfyed forbidding his

[1] 8th June, 1683. [2] 13th July, 1683.

personall presence) the other in person, signifying their purpose of marriage each with other, which being the first tyme they are desired to wait till the next Monthly Meeting, interim a certificate is ordered to be sent to signify the same to Hull Monthly Meeting.

The next Meeting is appointed to be at the house of Thomas Markham in Brigge.

Signed Robert Rockhill.

p. 109.

ATT a Monthly Meeting held at the house of Thomas Markham in Brigge the tenth day of the sixth month 1683[1] :—

This day Denis Marshall and Hannah Wake came into this Meeting the second time and signifyed the continuance of their purpose of marriage each with other, and brought a certificate from the Monthly Meeting in Holderness signifying the clearnes of all things on his part, and their unitye with their said pyrpose of marriage, wherewith wee having unitie also, have approved of the same & left the accomplishment thereof to their own conveniency.

Ordered that a contribution be collected in all the Perticuler Meetings belonging to this Monthly Meeting, and brought in to the next Monthly Meeting, whence the necessites of Friends being supplyed, the remainder to be sent up to the next Quarterly Meeting.

The next Monthly Meeting appointed at the house of Thomas Wresle in Boterwick.

Signed Robert Rockhill.

AT a Monthly Meeting held at the house of Thomas Wresle in Boterwick the 14th day of the 7th month 1683[2] :—

Contributions	Gainsburgh	00 : 12 : 04		
as followeth	Crowle ..	01 : 00 : 10	paid back	00 : 12 : 00
	Wintringham	00 : 18 : 00		
	Garthorp ..	00 : 11 : 00	paid back	00 : 05 : 00
	Brigg ..	00 : 14 : 00	to R. Ashton	
	old stock ..	00 : 03 : 02	in part of re-	
			pairs of Hally-	
		03 : 19 : 04	well house ..	01 : 05 : 06
				02 : 02 : 06

To be sent up to the Quarterly Meeting 01 : 16 : 10

[1] 10th August, 1683. [2] 14th September, 1683.

This day Robert Haslehurst of Hakeingthorp in the county of Darby, and Mary Potter of Lea in this county came into this Meeting & signified their purpose of marriage each with other, which being the first tyme they are desired to wait till the next Monthly Meeting. Interim a certificate thereof is ordered to be sent to the Monthly Meeting in Yorkshire.

The next Monthly Meeting ordered at the house of Thomas Markham in Brigge.

Signed Robert Rockhill.

At a Monthly Meeting held at the house of Thomas Markham the 12th day 8th month 1683[1] :—

This day Robert Haslehurst of Hackinthorpe abovesaid came into this Meeting the 2d tyme signifying the continuance of the purpose of marriage between him & Mary Potter of Lea, & brought a certificate from the Monthly Meeting at Warnsworth in Yorkshire signifying their satisfaction in the clearness of all things on his part and we being well satisfyed that all things are clear on her behalfe, have hereby signifyed our unitie with the same, and have left the consummation of their said purpose to their own conveniency according to the good order of Truth.

The next Monthly Meeting is appointed att the house of Thomas Wresle in Boterwick.

Signed Robert Rockhill.

p. 110.

At a Monthly Meeting held at the house of Thomas Wresle in Boterwick the ninth day of November 1683 :—

This day Benjamin Broadhead of Stockwith in the county of Nottingham and Mary Maw of Belton in the county of Lincolne came into this Meeting and signified their purpose of marriage each with other, which Friends of this meeting have taken notice of, and desired them to wait till the next Monthly Meeting, where they are to be present.

Ordered that a contribution be collected in all the severall Meetings & brought in to the next Monthly Meeting, whence Friends necessities being supplyed the rest to be sent to the Quarterly Meeting.

The next Meeting appointed at the house of Thomas Markham in Brigge.

Signed Robert Rockhill.

[1] 12th October, 1683.

At a Monthly Meeting held at the house of Thomas Markham in Brigge the 14th of December 1683 :—

Contributions came as followeth	Crowl ..	01 : 01 : 03	sent back	01 : 13 : 00
	Garthorp ..	00 : 11 : 06		
	Gainsburgh ..	00 : 09 : 09		00 : 12 : 11
	Wintringham	00 : 17 : 06		
	Brigg ..	00 : 16 : 00		00 : 18 : 00
		03 : 16 : 00	in all	03 : 03 : 11
	Rests in Thomas Markham's hand			00 : 12 : 01

This day Benjamin Broadhead of Stockwith in the county of Nottingham and Mary Maw of Belton in this county came into this meeting the second tyme, signifying the continuance of their purpose of marriage who finding all things clear on both parts have left the consummation thereof to their own conveniency, according to the good order of Truth.

The next Monthly Meeting to be at Brigge.

Signed Robert Rockhill.

At a Monthly Meeting held at the house of Thomas Markham in Brigg the 11 day of the 11 month 1683[1] :—

This day John Parsons of Brigg came into this Meeting and complained of severall injuries and wrongs, done unto him by Abraham Morrice of Lincolne, not only by reason of his gross breach of promisses, and confirmed engagements, but also by other indirect wayes and forged suggestions, to the great damage of him the said John Parsons as he alleadgeth, whereof this Meeting having taken notice, have ordered that Robert Rockhill draw up a few lines testifying the same to Friends of Lincoln Monthly Meeting & desire them to appoint a tyme & place convenient, when & where a select number of their Monthly Meeting, and the like number of ours may meet together to hear & determine the said Complaint (after a full hearing of both partyes) according to justice & righteousnes.

The next Monthly Meeting appointed to be at Brigge.

Signed Robert Rockhill.

p. 111.

At a Monthly Meeting held at the house of Thomas Markham in Brigge the eighth of the twelth month 1683[2] :—

Whereas it so falls out that the Quarterly Meeting at Lincolne will be kept before the ordinary time of our Monthly Meeting, it

[1] 11th January, 1684. [2] 8th February, 1684.

is ordered that such Friends as shall goe from each Particular Meeting upon the service of the Truth to the Quarterly Meeting, take with them their respective contributions, with an account of the wants of poor Friends in each meeting, and that they meet together so early at Lincolne as to dispatch the busines, before the Quarterly Meeting.

This day John Haslehurst of Gainsburgh came into this Meeting, & signifyed his intention of marriage with Mary Cliffe of Lincolne & brought a certificate under her hand testifying her consent to the same, which being the first time they are desired to wait till the next Monthly Meeting where they are both desired to be present.

Ordered that a contribution be collected in the severall Meetings belonging to this Monthly Meeting, and brought up to Lincoln the morning of the Quarterly Meeting whence the wants of poor Friends being supplyed, the rest to the Quarterly Meeting.

The next Monthly Meeting to be att Glamford bridge.

Signed Robert Rockhill.

At a Monthly Meeting held at the house of Thomas Markham in Glamfordbridge the 14 day of the first month 1683/4[1] :—

Contributions came in as followeth	Gainsburgh ..	00 : 10 : 10		s. d.
	Crowle ..	00 : 17 : 04	returnd	1 : 5
	Garthrop ..	00 : 11 : 06		
	Brigg ..	00 : 11 : 09		
	Wintringham	01 : 00 : 00		
		03 : 11 : 05		
To the Quarterly Meeting ..		02 : 00 : 00		
Reserved in Stock ..		01 : 10 : 00		

This day John Haslehurst of Gainsburgh came into this Meeting the 2d tyme, signifying the continuance of his purpose of marriage with Mary Cliffe of the citty of Lincolne, and brought a certificate from their Monthly Meeting at Welbourn certifying his and her appearance there & publication of their said purpose. Now, we knowing not any impedement on his part which may obstruct their proceedings, have here by signifyed our unity with the same, and left the consummation thereof to the further disquisition of Lincoln Monthly Meeting, & their own conveniency in the Truth.

The next Meeting appointed at the house of John Wresle in Thealbye.

Signed Robert Rockhill.

[1] 14th March, 1684.

At a Monthly Meeting held at the house of John Wresle in Thealby the 11 day 2d month 1684[1] :—

This day Michael Browne of Belton & Sarah Maw of Boterwick came into this Meeting & declared their purpose of marriage each with other, this Meeting have taken the same into consideration, and desired them to wait till the next Monthly Meeting where they are to be present.

The next Monthly Meeting appointed at the house of Robert Ashton in Eland.

Signed Robert Rockhill.

p. 112.

At a Monthly Meeting held at the house of Robert Ashton of Eland the 9th day of the 3d month 1684[2] :—

This day Michael Brown of Belton and Sarah Maw of Boterwick came into this Meeting the 2d tyme and signifyed the continuance of their purpose of marriage, which Friends have considered, and finding no impedement have unity with them and referre the consummation of their said purpose to their own conveniency, according to the good order of Truth.

This day William Hudson of Moorgate in the county of Nottingham, and Joan Codd of Thealby in this county came into this Meeting, and declared their purpose of marriage each with other, which this Meeting have taken into consideration and desired them to wait till the next Monthly Meeting where they are to be present.

Ordered that a contribution be collected in each particular Meeting and brought in to the next Monthly Meeting whence the wants of Friends being supplyed, the rest sent up to the Quarterly Meeting.

The next Meeting to be at Gainsburgh.

Signed R. Rockhill.

At a Monthly Meeting held at the house of Henry Sympson in Gainesburgh the 13 of the 4th month 1684[3] :—

Contributions came in thus	Crowle Meeting	01 : 04 : 00
	Gainsburgh	00 : 19 : 10
	Garthorp	00 : 18 : 10
	Wintringham..	01 : 06 : 04
	Brigg	01 : 01 : 00
		05 : 10 : 00
sent back by T. Wresle 10*s*.		
for the Quarterly Meeting if need be	.. ..	05 : 00 : 00

[1] 11th April, 1684. [2] 9th May, 1684. [3] 13th June, 1684.

This day William Hudson of Moorgate in the county of Nottingham & parish of Clareborough & Joan Codd of Thealby in this county came the 2d tyme into this Meeting declareing the continuance of their purpose of marriage, wherewith the meeting (knowing noe impediment on either side that may hinder their proceedings) are satisfyed, & hereby declare their Unity with their said purpose, and leave the consummation thereof to their own conveniency according to the good order of Truth.

The next Monthly Meeting appointed at the house of Edmond Morley in Adlingfleet. Signed Robert Rockhill.

p. 113.

At a Monthly Meeting held at the house of Edmond Morley in Adlingfleet the eleventh day of the fifth month 1684[1] :—

It is ordered that a contribution for the redemption of captives in Algieres be collected and brought to the next Monthly Meeting which is appointed at the house of Thomas Wrestle in West Boterwick. Signed Robert Rockhill.

At a Monthly Meeting of Friends at the house of Thomas Wrestle of Boterwick the 8th day of the 6th month 1684[2] :—

Contributions for the redemption of captives came in as followeth	Gainsburgh	00 : 09 : 09
	Garthorpe	00 : 11 : 00
	Wintringham	01 : 07 : 00
	Brigge	01 : 03 : 06
	Crowle	00 : 16 : 03
		04 : 07 : 06

Ordered that a contribution be collected against the next Monthly Meeting and brought in thither, whence the wants of Friends being supplyed, the rest brought up to the Quarterly Meeting.

The next Meeting is appointed at the house of Thomas Markham in Brigge. Signed Robert Rockhill.

At a Monthly Meeting held at the house of Thomas Markham in Brigge the 12th day of September 1684 :—

Contributions came in as followeth	Gainsburgh	00 : 11 : 00
	Garthorp	00 : 11 : 06
	Wintringham	00 : 15 : 06
	Crowle	00 : 15 : 00
	Brigge	00 : 14 : 00
	old stock	00 : 12 : 00
		03 : 19 : 00

[1] 7th July, 1684. [2] 8th August, 1684.

to Robert Ashton in full discharge of the repaires of Hallywell house	01 : 03 : 07
to be sent to the Quarterly Meeting	02 : 15 : 05

It is ordered by this Meeting that the severall persons who on the behalfe of their severall Meetings subscribed summes of mony for supply of George Nicholson's charge in his voyage, doe bring up those respective summs by them subscribed, to the next Monthly Meeting which is to be at the house of Thomas Wrestle in Boterwick.

Signed R. Rockhill.

At a Monthly Meeting held at the house of Thomas Wrestle in Boterwick the tenth day of the eighth month 1684[1] :—

Ordered by this Meeting that Thomas Wrestle lay downe money for the relief of a poor Friend belonging to their Meeting, and give an account thereof to the next Monthly Meeting, who will reimburse him.

Ordered that the next Monthly Meeting be held at the house of Thomas Markham in Brigge.

Signed Robert Rockhill.

p. 114.

At a Monthly Meeting held at the house of Thomas Markham in Brigg the Fourteenth day of November 1684 :—

Ordered that a contribution be collected in all the Perticuler Meetings, and brought in to the next Monthly Meeting, whence the wants of Friends being supplyed, the rest to be sent up to the next Quarterly Meeting.

Ordered that the next Monthly Meeting be att the house of Thomas Markham in Brigge.

Signed Robert Rockhill.

At a Monthly Meeting held at the house of Thomas Markham in Brigge the 12th day of the 10th month 1684[2] :—

Contributions came as follows	Gainsburgh Meeting	00 : 10 : 06
	Garthorp Meeting..	00 : 10 : 00
	Crowle Meeting	00 : 19 : 00
	Wintringham	00 : 17 : 00
	Brigge Meeting	00 : 14 : 00
		03 : 10 : 06

[1] 10th October, 1684. [2] 12th December, 1684.

sent back by J. Pilsworth .. .. 00 : 07 : 06
to Hester Stephenson .. .. 00 : 03 : 00
To be sent up to the Quarterly Meeting .. .. 02 : 10 : 00
Old stock in Thomas Markham's hand .. .. 01 : 10 : 00

This day William Browne of Belton and Mary Maw of the same came into this Meeting and signifyed their purpose of marriage each with other, which being the first tyme the Meeting hath recorded it and expects their presence at the next Monthly Meeting to receive Friends answere.

This day Robert Wilkinson of Wintringham & Elizabeth Pilesworth of Belton came into this Meeting & signifyed their purpose of marriage each with other, which being the first tyme the Meeting hath recorded it, expecting their presence at the next Monthly Meeting to receive Friends answere.

The next Monthly Meeting appointed at the house of Thomas Markham in Brigg. Signed Robert Rockhill.

At a Monthly Meeting held at the house of Thomas Markham in Brigge the 9th day of the eleventh month 1684[1] :—

This day William Browne of Belton & Mary Maw of the same came into this Meeting the second tyme to signify the continuance of their purpose of marriage, & all things being found cleare they have the approbation of this Meeting, and the consumation thereof is left to their own conveniency, according to the good order of Truth.

This day Robert Wilkinson came into this Meeting, and John Pilsworth on the behalfe of his daughter signifying the continuance of their purpose of marriage, who have the approbation of this likwise and the consumation thereof is left to their own conviency according to the good order of Truth.

Sent to Jane Carnell for her rent .. .. .. 00 : 05 : 00
to Anne Baines for her rent .. .. .. 00 : 04 : 00

p. 115.

Sent to Anne Baines & Anne[2] Carnels for their releife 00 : 05 : 00

The next Monthly Meeting to be at the house of Thomas Markham in Brigge. Signed Robert Rockhill.

At a Monthly Meeting held at the house of Thomas Markham in Brigge the 13 day of the 12 month 1684[3] :—

It is ordered by this Meeting that there be one large contribution collected and brought up to the next Monthly Meeting or to the Quarterly Meeting (which shall first happen) where Friends wants being supplyed, the rest to be given in to the Quarterly Meeting.

[1] 9th January, 1685. [2] *sic : recte* Jane. [3] 13th February, 1685.

The next Monthly Meeting to be at Thomas Wresles house in Boterwick.

Signed R. Rockhill.

At a Monthly Meeting appointed at Boterwick, but held at Lincolne the 10th day of the first month 1684/5[1] :—

Contributions as followeth	Brigg ..	01 : 00 : 00	sent back	00 : 02 : 11
	Crowle ..	01 : 01 : 00	sent back	00 : 07 : 06
	Gainsburgh ..	00 : 13 : 09	sent back	00 : 05 : 00
	Garthorp ..	00 : 12 : 00		
	Wintringham	01 : 08 : 02		00 : 14 : 11
		04 : 14 : 11	To the Quarterly Meeting ..	04 : 00 : 00

The next Meeting to be at Gainsburgh.

Signed Robert Rockhill.

At a Monthly Meeting held at the house of Henry Sympson in Gainsburgh the 10th day 2d month 1685[2] :—

There being no busines this Meeting the next Meeting is appointed at the house of John Wresle in Thealbye.

At a Monthly Meeting held at the house of John Wresle in Thealby the eighth day of the third month 1685[3] :—

The busines of Vincent Brownloe is referred to the next Monthly Meeting in the mean time Thomas Wresle is to enquire further of the matter, and give an account thereof.

It is ordered that a contribution be collected and brought into the next Monthly Meeting where Friends wants being supplyed, the remainder to be sent to the Quarterly Meeting.

The next Monthly Meeting appointed at the house of Robert Ashton in Ealand.

Signed Robert Rockhill.

p. 116.

At a Monthly Meeting held at the house of Robert Ashton in Ealand the 12th day of the fourth month 1685[4] :—

Contributions came in	00 : 11 : 04	Gainsburgh		
	00 : 19 : 09	Crowle	Garthorp	01 : 07 : 00
	00 : 00 : 00	Brigg	sent back to Crowle	00 : 12 : 00
	00 : 10 : 00	Garthorpe	Gainsburgh	00 : 05 : 00
	00 : 18 : 06	Wintringham		
				02 : 04 : 00
	02 : 19 : 07			
			Remaines	00 : 15 : 07

[1] 10th March, 1685. [2] 10th April, 1685. [3] 8th May, 1685.
[4] 12th June, 1685.

Thomas Wresle has made inquirie of Vincent Brownlow his busines and saith that divers things are still affirmed against him. Thomas Markham & William Smith are ordered by this Meeting to discourse Vincent about those things that are laid to his charge & give account thereof to the next Monthly Meeting, which is appointed at the house of Robert Reeder in Cottle Hall.

Signed R. Rockhill.

(NOTE.—At this point the Clerk was changed and the Minutes recommence at the other end of the Book, but there is no gap.)

p. 117.

ATT a Monthly Meeting held att Robert Reeders of Cottell Hall the 10th of 5th month 1685[1] :—

By order of the Quarterly Meeting Thomas Wresle was to pay unto John Pilsworth the sume of ten pounds : to reimburse the charge he was at with Margrey Fann : and the Quarterly Metting or Monthly Meeting will keepe Thomas Wresle indemnified. The next Monthly Meeting to be at Butterwick.

Signed per John Parsons.

ATT a Monthly Metting held at the house : Thomas Wresle of West Butterwicke the 14th of 6th month 1685[2] :—

Whereas John Garland has desarted the Mettings of Frinds Gods Truth, and has assembled hime selfe with the nashional way of worishep and some Friends haveing since spoaken with hime in refrence to his backe slideing and with all desiered to know the accasion to whome he haveing retorned no positive answer itt is ordred that Thomas Markham Henry Simson do speake to the said John, touching the same and give an account thereof to the next Monthly Metting.

It is ordred that the contrebushions be brought in to the next Mounthly Metting and the wants of each Perticler Metting being suplyed the remainder to be carried to the Quarterly Metting. The next Mounthly Metting to be at Brigg.

signed per John Parsons.

AT a Monthly Meeting held at the House of Thomas Markham of Brigg the 11th 7th mounth 1685[3] :—

The busnes touching John Garland is defered unto the next Mounthly Meeting.

[1] 10th July, 1685. [2] 14th August, 1685. [3] 11th September, 1685.

Contrebushions brought in	Gainsburgh	00 : 10 : 06
	Crowle	00 : 13 : 00
	Wintringham	01 : 01 : 06
	Garthrope	00 : 10 : 00
	Brigg	00 : 15 : 00
		03 : 10 : 00
retorned		
To Garthrope		00 : 16 : 00
Thomas Markham		00 : 06 : 08
Quarterly Meeting		02 : 07 : 04
		03 : 10 : 00

The next Mounthly Meeting to be at Thomas Wresles of Butterwicke.

p. 118.

Att a Mounthly Meeting held at the House of Thomas Wresle of West Butterwick the 9th of 8th mounth 1685[1] :—

This Meeting haveing bine acquanted : that William Vessey of Bellton hath gon from the truth and hath out of the Truth taken a wiffe by (or) before one called a lawles preste and also that John Urry of Epworth did countance and entertaine the said couple soe mareied, now Frends in this Metting in Gods feare doe condeme the afforsaid proseedings of the said William Vessey as euell and out of the Truth, as also John Urrys entertaing them there by seemeing to countance the same, itt is therefore ordred by this Metting that Thomas Wresle John Pilesworth & Robert Ashton doe speak unto the said persons that soe they may come to see the euell they have done and repent and turne unto the Lord and give an accout thereof unto the next Monthly Metting.

The busnes of John Garland is yett suspended.

The next Mounthly Meeting to be at Thomas Wresle of Buttrick.

Att a Mounthly Meeting held at the House of Thomas Wresle of West Butterwick the 13th of the ninthe mounth 1685[2] :—

Where as from the last Mounthly Meeting Thomas Wresle John Pilesworth and Robart Ashton was ordred to speake unto William Vessey who had taken a wiffe by on called a lawles preste and allso John Urry who entertained them there by semeing to incorage the same, now the said William Vessey and John Urry have this day bine in our Mounthly Meeting

[1] 9th October, 1685. [2] 13th November, 1685.

and have given testomonies of theire sorow and truble for what they have done and have condemned there afforesaid proseeding as unrightious and out of the Truth.

William Paine of West Butterwicke came into this Meeting to acquant them of his porpose of marrage with Kathren Johnson of Thealby who was also preasent itt being the furst time of thee of the same this Meeting hath taken itt into consereration untill the next Mounthly Meeting. The next Mounthly Meeting to be at Brigg.

Signed by John Parsons.

p. 119.

ATT a Monthly held at the house of Thomas Markham in Brigg the 11th 10th month 1685[1] :—

Contributions brought in from

	£	s.	d.
Crowle	00	15	10
Brigg	00	15	00
Wintringham	01	00	09
Gainsbrough	00	10	10
	03	02	05

Disbursments

	£	s.	d.
To Joseph Richardson ..	00	05	03
To Crowle for Ann Baines ..		07	02
to be sent to the Quarterly Meeting	02	10	00

This day William Pain and Katherim Johnson came into this Meeting the second time signifieing there continuance of there purpose of marrage and all things being clear of both parts Freinds doe give their approbation and leave the consumation thereof to there own convenience.

The next Meeting to be att Brigg.

ATT a Monthly Meeting at the house of Thomas Markham in Brigg the 8th day of the 11th month 1685/6[2] :—

The next Monthly Meeting ordred to be at the house of Thomas Markham in Brigg.

ATT a Monthly Meeting at the house of Thomas Markham in Brigg the 12 day of the 12 month 1685[3] :—

All things amongst us being well in order the next Monthly Meeting is appoynted att the house of Thomas Wresle in West Butterwick.

[1] 11th December, 1685. [2] 8th January, 1686. [3] 12th February, 1686.

Att a Monthly Meeting the house of Thomas Wresle in Butterwick the 12 day of the first month 1686[1] :—

Contributions brought in from	£	s.	d.
Crowle	01	08	00
Brigg	01	06	06
Wintringham	01	10	00
Gainsbrough	00	19	03
Garthorp	00	17	06
p. 120.	06	01	03
Toward the relief of the pore			
Sent to Brigg	01	05	09
sent to Crowle	00	15	06
sent to Garthorp	01	00	00
to be sent up to the Quarterly Meeting	03	00	00

This day Anthony Morrice of Thealby and Mary Wressle of the same came and declared there intentions of Marriage with each other & it being the first time it is left to the consideration of Freinds until the next Monthly Meeting where they are to be present.

The next Monthly Meeting to be att Ealand at the house of Robert Ashtons.

Att a Monthly Meeting held att the house of Robert Ashton of Ealand the 9th 2d month 1686[2] :—

This day Anthony Morrice came with Mary Wresle and published there intentions of marrage a second time according to the good order of Truth and all things being found clear on both sides the consummation of there said purpose is left to there own convenience.

The next Monthly Meeting to be held at the house of Henry Simpson in Gainsbrough.

Att a Monthly Meeting held at Henry Simpsons house in Gainsbrough the 14th 3d month 1686[3] :—

It is ordred that a larg contribution be collected and brought to the next Monthly Meeting.

All things being in good order amongst us it is ordred that the next Monthly Meeting be held at the house of John Wresle in Thealby.

Signed by Thomas Markham.

[1] 12th March, 1686. [2] 9th April, 1686. [3] 14th July, 1686.

p. 121.

Att a Monthly Meeting held at the house of John Wresle in Thealby the 11th 4th month 1686[1] :—

Contributions from the particular Meetings

	£	s.	d.
Imp. From Brigg Meeting	01	00	06
Crowle Meeting	00	19	09
Wintringham Meeting ..	01	04	00
Garthorp	00	12	06
Gainsbrough	00	15	06
	04	12	03
Returned back to Crowle ..	01	00	00
Returned back to Garthorp ..	00	12	03
sent up to the Quarterly Meeting	03	00	00

Edmond Morley is desired to lay down for this Meeting the sum of one pound eight pence unto Thomas Pepper for the keeping of a poor child and this Meeting will see him indemnified.

Whereas an account was given to this Meeting that some difference hath risen betwixt Thomas Markham of Brigg and John Dent of Roxby it is desired that Thomas Wresle of Wintringham doe speak with the said John Dent (Thomas Markham being present) that he with Thomas Wresle doe nominate persons time & place to hear & determine the said difference and the said Thomas Wresle is to give an account of ther proceedings therein to the next Monthly Meeting.

The next Monthly Meeting to be at Adlinfleet.

signed by Thomas Markham.

p. 122.

At a Monthly Meeting held at the house of Edmond Morley in Adlinfleet the 9th day of the 5th month 1686[2] :—

It is ordered that a contribution from severall services of the Truth be collected & brought up to the next Monthly Meeting.

The business betwixt John Dent & Thomas Markham is agreed before it came to the hearing of friends.

[1] 11th June, 1686. [2] 9th July, 1686.

It is ordered that the next Monthly Meeting be at the house of Thomas Wresle in Botterwick.

Signed by Joseph Richardson.

Att a Monthly Meeting held at the house of Thomas Wresle in Botterwick the 13th day of the 6th month 1686[1] :—

Contributions came in as followeth to be sent up to London for Truth service :

Crowle Meeting	00 : 17 : 06
Garthrop Meeting	00 : 09 : 00
Gainsburgh Meeting	00 : 12 : 10
Wintringham Meeting	1 : 1 : 0
Brigg Meeting	0 : 15 : 0
	3 : 15 : 4

This day came in George Frow of Burton Stather & declared his intentions of marriage with Mary Walker of Great Markham in the county of Nottingham, and brought a Certificate from Friends there signifying there satisfaction with the thing & Freinds here have taken it into there consideration till the next Monthly Meeting, where he is desired to be.

Ordered that a contribution be brought in to the next Monthly Meeting & Friends necessities be supplied out of it & the remainder be carried up to the Quarterly Meeting.

The next Monthly Meeting to be at the house of Thomas Markham in Brigg.

Signed by Joseph Richardson.

p. 123.

Att a Monthly Meeting held at the house of Thomas Markham in Brigg the 10th of the 7th month 1686[2] :—

Contributions came in as followeth :

		£ s. d.
Imp :	Gainsburgh Meeting ..	00 : 12 : 10
	Crowle Meeting	00 : 15 : 00
	Brigg Meeting	00 : 12 : 00
	Winteringam Meeting ..	01 : 00 : 02
	Garthrop Meeting	00 : 08 : 00
	added of stock left of old ..	00 : 08 : 06
	Totall	03 : 16 : 06

[1] 13th August, 1686. [2] 10th September, 1686.

Disbursements out of this as followeth :

	£	s.	d.
To Crowle Meeting ..	00 :	15 :	00
to Garthrop Meeting.. ..	00 :	10 :	00
to Edmond Morley more which he laid down ..	01 :	01 :	06
	02 :	06 :	06

Remaines to be carried to the Quarterly Meeting the sum of £01 : 10 : 00.

To Friends at London for Truths service 03 : 15 : 04.

This day George Frow of Burton upon Stather came the second time into the Monthly Meeting & declared the continuance of his intentions of marriage with Mary Walker of Great Markham, & brought a certificate from there Monthly Meeting, signifying her clearness from all other persons & Friends of this meeting knowing nothing to the contrary upon his account, have left the consumation thereof to there own discretion & conveniency according to the good order of Truth.

The next Monthly Meeting ordered to be at the house of Thomas Wresles in Botterwick.

Signed by Joseph Richardson.

p. 124.

Att a Monthly Meeting held at the house of Thomas Wresle in Botterwick the 8th day of the 8th month 1686[1] :—

No bussines appearing it was ordered the next Monthly Meeting ordered to be at the house of Thomas Markham in Brigge.

Att a Monthly Meeting held at the house of Thomas Markhams in Brigge the 12th day of the 9th month 1686[2] :—

It was ordered by this meeting that Thomas Wresle of Winteringham & Robert Wilkinson of the same, goe & speak to Margaret Hood of Whitton widdow, & admonish her to keep to the Truth, & to keep clear of letting out her affections towards marriage with any out of the Truth, that soe Truth & Freinds may not suffer by such disorderly practices, & bring in her answer to the next Monthly Meeting.

Whereas Thomas Wresle of Winteringham hath of late spoken to John Reeder of Winterton, belonging to the same Meeting, about his inclinations of taking to wife, one of the world's people, Freinds of this meeting has desired Thomas Wresle & David Crosby to goe once agains to him & advise & admonish him

[1] 8th October, 1686. [2] 12th November, 1686.

against such proceedings & practices, for the clearing of Truth & Freinds, & bring in his answer to the next Monthly Meeting.

Ordered that a contribution be collected & brought into the next Monthly Meeting—which is to be held at the house of Thomas Markham in Brigge.

Signed by Joseph Richardson.

Att a Monthly Meeting held at the house of Thomas Markham in Brigge the 10th day of the 10th month 1686[1] :—

Whereas Thomas Wresle of Winteringam & Robert Wilkinson of the same, was ordered by the last Monthly Meeting, to speak to Margret Hood of Whitton, about her goeing to marry with one of the world, they have accordingly done it, & thereby brought her to such a sence of Truth, as own that shee had done amiss, yet persistinge in the same has married him, but Freinds have cleared themselves & the Truth, by manifesting there disunion with all such practices.

Whereas David Crosby & Thomas Wresle has spoke the second time to John Reeder of Winterton, according to the order of the last Monthly Meeting, but thereby could make no impression upon him, for notwithstanding all the good advice & councell they gave him *(p. 125)* he would still goe endwaye & accomplished the same, contrary to Truth, however they have used there indeavour with him, in clearing Freinds & the Truth, which stands as a testimony against him and all others that shall be found in the like practices.

Contributions came in as followeth :		s.	d.
Gainsbrough		11	00
Crowle		15	03
Garthrop		10	00
Winteringam	01	01	00
Brigg	00	15	00
Totall	03	12	03

Disbursments as followeth for the necessities of the seaverall Meetings :

		s.	d.
To Thomas Wresle Botterwick ..		15	00
to Robert Reeder of Garthrop ..		10	00
to William Smith of Elsham ..		05	00
to Thomas Wresle Winteringam ..		02	03
Totall	01	12	03

	£	s.	d.
Remains to be sent up to the Quarterly Meeting ..	02	00	00

[1] 10th December, 1686.

This day Thomas Wresle of Botterwick published his intentions of marriage with Elizabeth Burton of Elletton in Yorkshire, & it being the first time, this Meeting desires him to wait there answer till the next Monthly Meeting which is to be at the house of Thomas Markham in Brigge.

Signed by Joseph Richardson.

ATT a Monthly Meeting held at the house of Thomas Markham in Brigg the 14th of the 11th month 1686[1] :—

This day Thomas Wresle of Botterwick came the 2d time into our Monthly Meeting, & declared the continuance of his intentions of marriage, with Elizabeth Burton of Elleton & brought a certificate with him from there Monthly Meeting, & we finding all things clear on his part, have left the consumation thereof to her & Freinds of that Meeting, according to the good order of Truth.

Ordered that a contribution be collected & brought to the next Monthly Meeting.

The next Meeting to be held at Thomas Markhams in Brigge.

Signed by Joseph Richardson.

p. 126.

ATT a Monthly Meeting held at the house of Thomas Markham in Brigge the 11th of the 12th month 1686[2] :—

Contributions came in as followeth :

	£	s.	d.
Gainsbrough	00	10	03
Crowle	00	13	00
Garthrop	00	10	00
Wintringham	00	17	09
Brigg	00	15	00
	03	06	00

	£	s.	d.
Disburst to Edmond Morley for Garthrop Meeting..		18	00
to Edmond Morley more for Robert Pickhaver boy		10	00
To Thomas Wresle for Crowle Meeting.. ..		10	00
to Joseph Richardson for Brigg Meeting		05	00
To Thomas Wresle Botterwick more for Happy Browne		10	00
Totall	02	10	00
Remaines yet in stock undisposed	00	16	00

[1] 14th January, 1687. [2] 11th February, 1687.

Ordered that another contribution be collected for the service of the Quarterly Meeting & brought into the next Monthly Meeting which is to be at the house of Thomas Wresles in Botterwick.

Signed by Joseph Richardson.

Att a Monthly Meeting held at the house of Thomas Wresle in Botterwick the 4th of the first month 87[1] :—

Collections came in as followeth :

Gainsbrough ..	10 : 06		
Crowle ..	15 : 00		
Wintringam ..	18 : 00		
Brigg	15 : 02		s.
Garthrop ..	08 : 00	In stock before	16
			£ s. d.
Totall ..	03 : 06 : 08	Sent to the Quarterly Meeting	04 : 00 : 00
		Remains in Joseph Richardson hands ..	00 : 02 : 08

The next Monthly Meeting to be at the house of Henry Sympsons in Gainsbrough.

Signed by Joseph Richardson.

p. 127.

Att a Monthly Meeting held at the house of Henry Symsons of Gainsbrough the 8th of the 2d month 87[2] :—

Freinds of this meeting being informed that Mary Cod, who was put forth as an apprentice, untill she came to 18 years old, that now the time is near expired, & shee still left to Freinds care.

Ordered that a contribution be collected & brought into the next Monthly Meeting, which is to be at John Wresles of Thealby.

Signed by Joseph Richardson.

Att a Monthly Meeting held at the house of John Wresles in Thealby the 13th day of the 3d month 1687[3] :—

It is desired by Friends at this Meeting to inquire for a convenient place for Mary Codd, who is still at Friends care : & to be ordered as may be seen meet.

[1] 4th March, 1687. [2] 8th April, 1687. [3] 13th May, 1687.

Contributions came in as followeth:

	£ s. d.		s. d.
Gainsbrough ..	00 : 11 : 06		
Crowle	00 : 12 : 00		
Garthrop	00 : 09 : 00		
Wintringham ..	00 : 14 : 00		
Brigg	00 : 13 : 00		
	————	Disburst to Crowle Meeting	10 : 00
	02 : 19 : 06	to Brigg Meeting	20 : 00

Remains in Stock yet 01 : 09 : 06

This day Will West of Gateburton came into the meeting & published his intentions of marriage with Mary Box of Harlinton, and brought with him a certificate from there Monthly Meeting signifying her consent thereto & this being the first time, they are desired to wait Freinds answer till next Monthly Meeting.

This day Thomas Browne West Botterwick came into the Monthly Meeting & published his intentions of marriage with Elizabeth Margrave of Belton, they being both present & it being the first time they are desired to wait Friends answer till next Monthly Meeting.

This day John Pilsworth of Epworth came into the Monthly Meeting & published his intentions of marriage with Mary Everatt of Pontefract in Yorkshire, & this being the first time he is desired to wait friends answer till next Monthly Meeting.

This day Anthony Godfrey of Luddinton came into our Meeting & published his intentions of marriage with Mary Reeder of Cotley Hall, they both being present & this being the first time they are desired to wait friends answer till next Monthly Meeting where they are to be personally present.

p. 128.

It is desired that a contribution be brought into the next Monthly Meeting which is to be at Edmond Morleys in Adlinfleet.

Signed by Joseph Richardson.

Att a Monthly Meeting held at the house of Edmund Morley in Adlinfleet the 11th of the 4th month 1687[1] :—

It is concluded betwixt Freinds of this Meeting & John Howell, taylor in Brigg that the said John Howell shall take Hester Stephenson son of Elsham an apprentice, for the terme of nine yeare, & he to finde the said boy all things excepting shirts & stockings which his mother is to find or if shee be not in abillity then Friends will doe it for her, & the said John

[1] 11th June, 1687.

Howell is to have with him of Friends, four pound ten shillings in money after the indentures be sealed to be paid fifty shillings the first yeare & forty shillings the next.

Contributions came in as followeth :

			£ s. d.
		Wintringham	00 : 15 : 00
		Gainsbrough	00 : 10 : 10
	£ s. d.	Crowle ..	00 : 12 : 00
paid of it to Edmond Morley	01 : 05 : 0	Brigg ..	00 : 14 : 00
paid Thomas Wresle of it ..	00 : 05 : 4	Garthrop ..	00 : 09 : 00
Remines yet	01 : 10 : 06		
left in Stock before ..	01 : 09 : 06	Totall ..	03 : 00 : 10

	£ s. d.
The whole to be carried up to the Quarterly Meeting is	03 : 00 : 00

This day William West of Gateburton came into this Meeting & signified the continuance of his intentions of marriage with Mary Box of Harlinton & brought a certificate from the Monthly Meeting at Balby that all things is clear on her part & we knowing nothing but all things is clear on his part have left the consumation thereof to there own discretion & conveniency according to the good order of Truth.

This day Thomas Browne Botterwick & Elizabeth Margrave of Belton came the second time into our Meeting & signified the continuance of there intention of marriage, and all things being found clear on both parties the consumation is left to there own convenience according to Truth order.

This day Anthony Godfrey of Luddinton & Mary Reeder of Colley Hall came into our Meeting the second time & signified there continuance of intentions of marriage, & all friends being satisfied have left the consumation thereof to there own convenience.

This day John Pilsworth of Epworth came the 2d time into our Meeting signified the continuance of his purpose of marriage with Mary Everatt of Pomfract & brought a certificate from them to signify her clearness from all others persons, friends here knowing nothing on the contrary on his part have left the consumation thereof to there own convenience according to the good order of Truth.

This day Francis Dent of Thealby came into the Monthly Meeting & published his intentions of marriage with Anna Everatt of Lincoln, & brought with him a few lines signifying her willingness, this being the first time, they are desired to wait Friends answer till next Monthly Meeting, which is to be at David Crosby house in Gunhouse.

Signed by Joseph Richardson.

p. 129.

ATT a Monthly Meeting held at the house of David Crosby in Gunhouse the 8th of the 5th month 1687[1] :—

This day Mary Codd came under the consideration of this Meeting, & it is desired that some care be taken about the disposing of her, to some place against the next Monthly Meeting, & to search the regester when her time with John Potter is expired.

This day Francis Dent came into the Meeting but no further progress being made in that concern, they are at liberty one from the other.

The next Monthly Meeting to be at the house of Thomas Wresles in Botterwick.

Signed by Joseph Richardson.

ATT a Monthly Meeting held at the house of Thomas Wresles in Botterwick the 12th of the 6th month 1687[2] :—

The disposing of Mary Codd is deferred till the next Monthly Meeting.

It is ordered that a contribution be brought in to the next Monthly Meeting which is ordered to be at the house of John Pilsworth in Belton.

Signed by Joseph Richardson.

ATT a Monthly Meeting held at the house of John Pilsworth in Belton the 9th of the 7th month 1687[3] :—

It is ordered by this Meeting that Mary Codd be brought to Jane Davis of Belton by Gainsbrough friends at there conveniency.

Contributions came in as followeth :

	£	s.	d.
Gainsbrough	00 :	15 :	00
Crowle	00 :	13 :	06
Garthrop	00 :	10 :	00
Winteringham	00 :	17 :	00
Brigge	00 :	14 :	06
Totall	03 :	10 :	00

	s.	d.
Disburst to Epworth Meeting ..	05 :	00
to Garthrop Meeting ..	15 :	00

	£	s.	d.
Remained to be sent up to the Quarterly Meeting	02 :	10 :	00

Ordered that the next Monthly Meeting be held at the house of Thomas Markham in Brigge.

Signed by Joseph Richardson.

[1] 8th July, 1687. [2] 12th August, 1687. [3] 9th September, 1687.

p. 130.

Att a Monthly Meeting held at the house of Thomas Markham in Brigg the 14th of the 8th month 1687[1] :—

No business appearing the next Monthly Meeting is ordered to be at the house of Thomas Wresles in Botterwick.

Signed by Joseph Richardson.

Att a Monthly Meeting held at the house of Thomas Wresles in Botterwick the 11th day of the 9th month 1687[2] :—

It was ordered that a contribution be collected & brought in to the next Monthly Meeting, which is to be at the house of Thomas Markhams in Brigg.

Signed by Joseph Richardson.

Att a Monthly Meeting held at the house of Thomas Markhams in Brigg the 9th of the 10th month 1687[3] :—

Contributions came in as followeth :

		s.	d.
Gainsbrough		13 :	4
Crowle			
Garthrop		09 :	0
Winteringham ..		14 :	10½
Brigg		13 :	06
	s.	02 : 10 :	8½
Disburst to Thomas Pepper	15 : 0		
To Gainsbrough for Mary Codd	4 : 6		
	Rest	01 : 11 :	02½

The next Monthly Meeting ordered to be at the house of Thomas Markhams in Brigge.

Signed by Joseph Richardson.

Att a Monthly Meeting held at the house of Thomas Markham in Brigge the 13th of the 11th month 1687[4] :—

The contribution for William Birket & other necessary charges came in as followeth :

		£	s.	d.
Imp.	from the Quarterly Meeting	06 :	00 :	00
	from Gainsbrough Meeting	01 :	00 :	00
	from the Ile Meeting ..	01 :	00 :	00
	from Winteringham Meeting	01 :	12 :	00
	from Brigge Meeting ..	01 :	10 :	00
	from Garthrop Meeting ..	00 :	09 :	00
In stock from Quarterly Meeting			16 :	00

Totall 12 : 07 : 00.

[1] 14th October, 1687. [2] 11th November, 1687. [3] 9th December, 1687.
[4] 13th January, 1688.

p. 131.

Disposed to William Birket, for the supplying his nessessity at present, for the which he gives his own bond to pay it againe, when the Lord shall inable him, the sum of £ s. d. 10 00 00

The bond is made to Henry Symson of Gainsbrough for the use of Freinds.

Disbursed to Thomas Pepper for close & other nessesaries for a boy put apprentice to him by Freinds .. £01 : 00 : 02

Rests in stock .. .. 01 : 06 : 10

Freinds are desired to bring account of there sufferings for tythe & other things to the next Monthly Meeting that care may be taken to send them to John Whitehead in due time.

The next Monthly Meeting to be at Thomas Markhams house in Brigg.

Signed by Joseph Richardson.

ATT a Monthly Meeting held at the house of Thomas Markhams in Brigge the 10th of the 12th month 87[1] :—

An account of sufferings was inquired after & ordered to be made ready to send up to Lincolne to John Whitehead in due time.

Ordered that a contribution be collected & brought to the next Monthly Meeting which is to be at Thomas Wresles in Botterwick.

Signed by Joseph Richardson.

THE Monthly Meeting falling for conveniency sake to be at Lincolne the 7th of the first month 1687/8[2] :—

Contributions came in as followeth :

	£ s. d.
from Gainsbrough	00 : 12 : 06
Crowle	00 : 11 : 06
Winteringham	00 : 19 : 00
Brigge	00 : 13 : 00
Totall	02 : 16 : 00
Disburst to Thomas Wresle for the Ile charges	00 : 16 : 00
for Quarterly Meeting	02 : 00 : 00
Laid down at Quarterly Meeting more	06 : 06

Rests yet in the Monthly Meeting stock 01 : 00 : 04.

[1] 10th February, 1688. [2] 7th March, 1688.

Sufferings being this day made inquiry after are not yet found in order soe are ordered not to faile to get them ready against next Monthly Meeting, which is to be at Thomas Wresle in Botterwick.

Signed by Joseph Richardson.

p. 132.

Att a Monthly Meeting held at the house of Thomas Wresles in Botterwick the 13th day of the 2d month 1688[1] :—

Sufferings for tythe & other things, came into this Meeting and was ordered to be sent to John Whitehead.

Brought into this Meeting an account of Garthrop contribution which should have come to the last, being 8*s.* 6*d.* which was given to Thomas Pepper of Ustflet for & towards the maintenance of John Pickhaver as was agreed by friends.

	£	s.	d.
There rested in Joseph Richardson hands in Stock	00 :	15 :	4
Disburst at this Meeting to Anthony Morrice for the releife of Widdow Carnell the sum of ..	00 :	05 :	00
& to Joseph Richardson for close for John Pickhaver that lives with Thomas Pepper, being the remainder of the stock	00 :	10 :	4

The next Monthly Meeting ordered to be at Henry Simson house in Gainsbrough.

Att a Monthly Meeting held at the house of Henry Simsons in Gainsbrough the 11th of the 3d month 1688[2] :—

It is agreed upon & consented unto by friends of this Meeting that John Howell, taylor in Brigg shall have with Ester Stephenson son Joseph, the sum of three pound & fourteen shillings, to be paid one half the first yeare & the other the yeare following.

It is ordered by this Meeting that care be taken for the tabling of Mary Codd, who is at present with Jane Davis of Belton

The case of Appelline Brown of Crowle is to be considered & given an account of by Thomas Wresle of Botterwick to the next Monthly Meeting.

It is ordered a contribution be collected & brought into the next Monthly Meeting which is to be at the house of John Wresle in Thealby.

[1] 13th April, 1688. [2] 11th May, 1688.

At a Monthly Meeting held at the house of John Wresle in Thealby the 8th day of the 4th month 1688[1] :—

Contributions came in as followeth :

p. 133.

	s. d.		£ s. d.
Gainsbrough ..	13 : 00		
Butterwick ..	14 : 00		
Brigge	15 : 00	Totall ..	03 : 05 : 00
Winteringham ..	14 : 00		
Garthrop ..	09 : 00		

Disposed to Butterwick Meeting for Mary Codd..	00 : 15 : 00
to Garthrop Meeting for John Pickhaver..	00 : 10 : 00
To be carried up to the Quarterly Meeting	02 : 00 : 00

Agreed by this Meeting that John Pickhaver who now lives wth Thomas Pepper of Usflet is to be apprenticed eight yeares with Michaell Beacock of Keadby, taylor, & this Meeting doth promiss to pay him £5, to be paid 40*s* the first year 40*s* the second year & 20*s* the third year, & the said Michaell Beacock is to finde him all things necessary whatsoever, & to be alikeing till next Monthly Meeting.

The next Monthly Meeting to be at Robert Reeders of Cotley Hall.

Att a Monthly Meeting held at the house of Robert Reeders in Cotley Hall the 14th of the 5th month 1688[2] :—

As to Michaell Beacok takeing John Pickhaver apprentice, it being neglected since last Monthly Meeting, he is to take him from this alikeing till the next Monthly Meeting where they are both desired to appear in order to conclude that matter.

Ordered that a contribution be collected & brought up to the next Monthly Meeting which is to be at David Crosbys of Gunhouse.

Att a Monthly Meeting held at the house of David Crosbys in Gunhouse the 10th of the 6th month 1688[3] :—

Michaell Beacok came wth John Pickhaver to the Meeting, where the boy declared his unwillingness to live with him : soe was ordered to Robert Reeder of Cotley Hall.

Contributions came in as follows :

Brigg	00 : 13 : 6
Wintringham	00 : 12 : 0
Crowle	00 : 10 : 6
Gainsbrough	00 : 10 : 4
Garthrop	00 : 8 : 6
	2 : 14 : 10

[1] 8th June, 1688. [2] 14th July, 1688. [3] 10th August, 1688.

Disbursments	To Joseph Richardson		11 : 03
	to Thomas Wresle Botterwick ..		8 : 6
	To Thomas Pepper		1 : 00 : 00
	to Michael Beacok		00 : 06 : 00
Rest in Joseph Richardson hand			09 : 00

Next Meeting at Thomas Wresles Butterwick.

p. 134.

ATT a Monthly Meeting held at the house of Thomas Wresles in Butterwick the 14th day of the 7th month 1688[1] :—

It is ordered that Thomas Wresle John Pilsworth & Robert Berrier doe take notice of the condition of Widdow Browne of Crowle, & minister to her nessesity accordingly, & this Meeting will see them indemnified.

It is ordered that Thomas Wresle John Pilsworth & Robert Berrier know of Jane Davisson what shee hath received for keeping of Mary Codd that what is wanting to her for that service may be speedily paid her & to give an account to the next Monthly Meeting.

It is ordered by this meeting that the first bargaine stand betwixt Michaell Beacock of Kidby & John Pickhaver & that indentures be made ready against the next meeting for the same purpose.

It is ordered that a contribution be collected & brought up to the next Meeting which is to be at Brigg.

ATT a Monthly Meeting held at Brigg the 12th day of the 8th month 1688[2] :—

Contributions came in as followeth :

	£	s.	d.
Crowle	00 :	14 :	4
Gainsbrough	00 :	12 :	6
Winteringham	00 :	18 :	6
Brigg	00 :	13 :	6
Garthrop	00 :	09 :	0
In Stock	00 :	09 :	00
Totall ..	03 :	16 :	10
Sent to the Quarterly Meeting ..	03 :	00 :	00
Rests in Joseph Richardson hand ..	00 :	16 :	10

An account came into this meeting that Thomas Wresle of Butterwick has agreed with Jane Davis of Belton to keep her for fifteene pence a week (that is Mary Codd) who has been already

[1] 14th September, 1688. [2] 12th October, 1688.

with her a yeare the 16th day of the 7th month last 1688[1] and that shee had had towards that charge bott 01 : 10 : 00.

Disburst at this meeting for Jane Davis of Belton upon the account of Mary Codd out of the Stock 00 : 15 : 00
Rests yet in Stock .. .. .. 00 : 01 : 10

The case of Widdow Browne of Crowle came under consideration & the Ile friends are desired to lye down 5*s* towards the suplying her present nessesity & to be paid agains the next Monthly Meeting.

p. 135.

Ordered that a contribution be collected & brought to the next Monthly Meeting which is to be att Brigg.

A testimony writt by Ann Everatt condemning her carrige & proceedings with Francis Dent of Thealby.

To the Monthly Meeting of Freinds belonging to Brigge Meeting.

Dear Freinds whereas there was formerly an intention of marriage depending between Francis Dent of Thealby & my self, yet nevertheless being perswaded thereto by my mother, beyond my own clearness or freedome, therefore for the prevention of future sufferings, either to the said Francis Dent or my selfe I broke of from him in an unadvised manner, & hath been much greived, that ever I gave Francis such occasion against me as he has had for the Truth sake. And further I doe hereby Certify unto you my friends or unto whomsoever it may concern, that Francis Dent aforesaid is free & clear from me, as concerning any thing in relation to marrige or any such covenant and is free to make his choyce otherwise as the Lord may please to order & guide him, witness my hand this 26 day of the 4th month at Lincolne in the year 1688.

Anna Everatt.

Att a Monthly Meeting held at Brigg the 9th of 9th month 1688[2] :—

Contributions came in as followeth :

	£	s.	d.
Crowle	00 :	12 :	6
Gainsbrough	00 :	13 :	0
Winteringham	00 :	13 :	0
Brigg	00 :	13 :	0
Garthrop	00 :	09 :	0
Totall ..	03 :	00 :	6

[1] 16th September, 1688. [2] 9th November, 1688.

	£	s.	d.	
To Michaell Beacok	00	12	9	for Pickhaver repaires
To Thomas Wresle Botterwick ..	01	00	0	for Jane Davis of Belton
To Thomas Wresle of Botterwick	00	10	00	for Happy Brown & James Dixon
To Joseph Richardson	00	14	0	for Pickhaver Close
Rests in Stock	00	05	7	in Joseph Richardson hand

p. 136.

Ordered that a contribution be collected & brought up to the next Monthly Meeting.

It is desired by Friends of this Meeting that care be take in every Perticular Meeting to bring in account of what they have suffered in tythe either by priest or impropriator.

It is ordered the next Monthly Meeting be at Brigge.

Att a Monthly Meeting held at Brigg the 14th of the 10th month 88[1] :—

The account not being perfected of Freinds sufferings for tythe, are referred till the next Monthly Meeting where Friends are desired to bring them in.

Contributions came in as followeth :

		£	s.	d.
Imps.	Gainsbrough	00	13	6
	Crowle	00	12	0
	Winteringham	00	15	3
	Brigg	00	12	00
	Garthrop	00	08	06
	Totall	03	01	03
	In Stock ..	00	05	07

	£	s.	d.
Disburst to John Orre for the girl with Jane Davis of Belton a paire of shoes	00	02	0
To John Howill towards his apprentice	01	00	0
To the Quarterly Meeting	02	00	0
Rests in Stock	00	04	10

Lenord Bainton of Frodingham came into this Meeting & published his intentions of marriage with Deborah Fichett of the same

[1] 14th December, 1688.

shee being present gave her consent, it being the first time they are desired to wait for answer till the next Monthly Meeting, where they are both desired to be.

The next Monthly Meeting to be at Brigge.

p. 137.

ATT a Monthly Meeting held at Brigg the 11th of the 11th month 1688[1] :—

Friends are desired to make ready there accounts of suffering upon the account of tythe or other things & send them speedily away before the next Monthly Meeting that they may be sent to John Whitehead at Fiskerton in due time.

Ordered that a contribution be collected & brought up to the next Monthly Meeting.

Ordered that the next Monthly Meeting be at Brigge.

ATT a Monthly Meeting held at Brigge the 8th day of the 12th month 1688[2] :—

Friends have brought into this Meeting an account of there suffering by tythe & ordered them to be farely written & sent to John Whithead the first opportunity.

Contributions came in as followeth :

	£ s. d.
Gainsbrough	00 : 13 : 0
Crowle	00 : 13 : 10
Brigge	00 : 14 : 06
Wintringham	00 : 13 : 0
Garthrop	00 : 08 : 0
Totall ..	03 : 02 : 04
from the Quarterly Meeting ..	00 : 19 : 00
In stock more	00 : 04 : 10
Totall ..	04 : 06 : 02

Disburst to John Howell of Brigg .. 00 : 17 : 00
which makes up half the money of £3 : 14 he is to have with Ester Stevenson son of Elsham.

	£ s. d.
Disburst to John Pilsworth for Jane Davis of Belton for the use of Mary Codd which is towards this last year beginning the 16th day of the 7th month 1688[3].	01 : 00 : 00

[1] 11th January, 1689. [2] 8th February, 1689. [3] 16th September, 1688.

	£	s.	d.
Disburst to Michaell Beacok towards what he is to have with his apprentice John Pickhaver by Joseph Richardson	01	00	00

p. 138.

	£	s.	d.
Disburst to Robert Berrier for the present releif of Widdow Brown his neighbour the sum ..	01	00	00
Disburst to Robert Berrier for the necessity of Cassandra Chapman the sum of	00	05	00
Disburst to William Smith for releif of Mary Goxhill	00	02	06
Disburst to William Smith of Elsham for the releif of Hester Stevenson (soe that nothing remains in Stock)	00	01	08

Lenord Bainton of Frodingham & Deborah Fitchett of the same came the second tyme into this Meeting & signified the continuance of there intentions of marriage each with other & Friends having nothing against it, have left the consumation thereof to there own conveniency acording to the good order of Truth.

Edward Markwell of Brigg & Elizabeth Richardson of the same came into this Meeting & published there intentions of marriage each with other & it being the first time they are desired to wait Friends answer till the next Monthly Meeting.

John Howell of Brigge came into this meeting & published his intentions of marriage with Mary Dent of Thealby & shee being present gave her consent it being the first time they are desired to wait Friends answer till the next Monthly Meeting.

Ordered that a contribution be collected & brought into the next Monthly Meeting which is to be held at Brigge.

Att a Monthly Meeting held at Brigg the 8th day of the first month 1689[1] :—

Contributions came in as followeth :

	£	s.	d.
Gainsbrough	00	12	10
Crowle	00	10	06
Brigge	00	14	00
Winteringham	00	14	00
Garthrop	00	08	00
	02	19	04

[1] 8th March, 1689.

p. 139.

Ordered that forty shillings by carried up to the Quarterly Meeting & twenty shillings more be paid to Michaell Beacock which will be in full for the first year.

Whereas it came under consideration in this Meeting about the Settlement of a Woemans Meeting and alsoe of setling the Monthly Meeting at Brigg, except occasions of Truth require it elswhere. Freinds are desired to acquaint each Perticular Meeting therewith & bring in there answer to the next Monthly Meeting.

This day Edward Markwell of Brigge came a second time into our Meeting & signified the continuance of his purpose of marriage with Elizabeth Richardson of the same: & all things being found clear on the behalf of both parties the consumation thereof is left to themselves according to the good order of Truth.

This day John Howell of Brigg came a second time into the Meeting & signified the continuance of his purpose of marriage with Mary Dent of Thealby: and all things being found clear on the behalf of both parties, the consumation thereof is left to themselves & relations concernd, according to the good order of Truth.

This day William Harrison of Winteringham came into our Meeting & published his intentions of marriage with Susanna Browne of Epworth and shee being present gave her consent it being the first time: they are desired to wait Freinds answer till the next Monthly Meeting.

This day Joseph Langley of Elletton in the county of Yorke came into our Meeting & published his intentions of marriage with Sarah Westoby daughter of Anthony Westoby, senr., of Winteringham in the county of Lincolne & shee being present gave her consent which being the first time they are desired to wait Friends answer till the next Monthly Meeting.

This day Joseph Wresle of Roxby came into our Meeting & published his intentions of marriage with Elizabeth Turner of Winteringham & shee being present gave her consent, it being the first time they are both desired to wait Friends answer till the next Monthly Meeting.

p. 140.

That whereas William Harrison & Susanna Browne has an intention of marriage each with other, shee being a widdow & has children left her by a former husband they have both joyntly chosen Thomas Wresle of Botterwick & Thomas Wresle of Winteringham, to set out what portions her children shall have more than was given by there father last will, & give an account to the next Monthly Meeting, which is to be at Thomas Wresles in Botterwick.

signed by Joseph Richardson.

Att a Monthly Meeting held at the house of Thomas Wresles in Botterwick the 12th day of the 2d month 1689[1] :—

Freinds of this Meeting having taken into consideration what was proposed the last Monthly Meeting, touching the setlement of a Woemans Meeting for these parts of the county have generally consented & agreed for it to be held where the Monthly Meeting is thought fitt to be kept.

Whereas Thomas Wresle of Botterwick & Thomas Wresle of Winteringham was ordered by the last Monthly Meeting, to see what Susanna Browne of Epworth was willing to setle upon her two sons in the time of her widdowhood, they accordingly went & shee agreed to give, & William Harrison her intended husband consented, that the elder son John Browne, should have fifteene pounds & the younger son Thomas Browne should have twenty pounds, which Thomas Wresle of Botterwick is desired to see confirmed before marriage, & the money to be paid to them when they shall attaine the age of twenty one yeares, & if either of them dye the survivor is to have his brothers part & neither of them to be accountable for there table provided they carry themselves as they ought to doe to there parents.

The state & condition of Happy Browne widdow in Ealand came under consideration in this Meeting, & Freinds have desired Thomas Wresle, William Browne, John Pilsworth & Robert Berrier to goe to her & see what is needfull to be done for her: and bring an account to the next Monthly Meeting.

This day William Harrison of Winteringham & Susanna Browne of Epworth came a second tyme into the Meeting, & signified the continuance of there purpose of marriage each with other, & no objection appearing to hinder there said intentions, Freinds of this meeting have left the consumation thereof to themselves with the advice of Freinds according to the good order of Truth.

This day Joseph Langley of Elloughton & Sarah Westoby of Winteringham came a second tyme into our Meeting & signified the continuance of there purpose (*p. 141*) of marriage each with other, & brought a certificate from the Monthly Meeting to which he does belong, signifieing his clearness & Freinds consent to the purpose aforesaid. And Freinds in this meeting findeing

[1] 12th April, 1689.

nothing but clearness on her part have given there consent, & left the consumation thereof to themselves with Freinds advise according to the good order of Truth.

This day Joseph Wresle of Roxby, & Elizabeth Turner of Winteringham came a second tyme into our Meeting & signified the continuance of there purpose of marriage each with other & Freinds finding nothing to hinder there said proceedings have left the consumation thereof to themselves with the advice of Freinds according to Truths order.

In regard that Freinds of this meeting have agreed to the setlement of a Woemans Meeting in these parts of the county, it is desired by Friends that care be taken to meet together by the 10th houre of the day that no Freinds be straitned to get home in due tyme.

The next Monthly Meeting to be at Henry Sympsons house in Gainsbrough.

Signed by Joseph Richardson.

Att a Monthly Meeting held at the house of Henry Sympsons in Gainsbrough the 10th day of the 3d month 1689[1] :—

Whereas Thomas Wresle, William Browne, John Pilsworth & Robert Berrier was desired by the last Monthly Meeting to inspect the condition of Happy Browne widdow in Ealand, they have accordingly done it, & judges her necessity to stand in need of five pound supply, which is to be laid before the next Quarterly Meeting at Lincolne.

Ordered that a contribution be collected & brought up to the next Monthly Meeting, which is to be at David Crosby house in Gunhouse.

Signed by Joseph Richardson.

p. 142.

Att a Monthly Meeting held at the house of David Crosby in Gunhouse the 14th of the 4th month 1689[2] :—

Ordered by this meeting that Thomas Wresle, William Browne, John Pilsworth & Robert Berrier, take care of the goods of Happy Browne of Ealand lately deceased, & advise with some of the most sober inhabitants about paying her debts & putting her children forth, & bring an account thereof to the next Monthly Meeting.

Thre of Widdow Brownes children is left with Robert Berrier of Ealand till further order & Freinds will consider him for them.

[1] 10th May, 1689. [2] 14th June, 1689.

Contributions came in as followeth:

	£	s.	d.
Gainsbrough	00	19	10
Crowle	01	09	09
Winteringham	01	03	01
Brigge	01	06	00
Garthrop	00	11	00
Totall ..	05	00	8
In Stock ..	01	19	00

Disbursments are out of it as followeth:

	£	s.	d.
Imp: To Thomas Wresle for Jane Davis Belton ..	00	15	00
To William West Gainsbrough for poor Friends	00	02	06
To Thomas Wresle for releife of Jane Carnell	00	05	00
To William Browne for releife of Cass: Chapman	00	05	00
To Thomas Wresle Winteringham for a Friend coffin (that dyed)	00	06	08
	01	14	2
Ordered to the Quarterly Meeting	05	00	00
Rests in stock	00	05	06

The next Monthly Meeting ordered to be at John Wresles house in Thealby.

Signed by Joseph Richardson.

Att a Monthly Meeting held at the house of John Wresle in Thealby the 12th of the 5th month 1689[1] :—

According to the order of the last Monthly Meeting Thomas Wresle, William Browne, John Pilsworth & Robert Berrier gives an account to this Meeting that they have spoken to the inhabitants of Crowle, about Happy Browne children, & they are willing to allow something towards the charge of there Education, but has not yet determined what, in the mean time this meeting orders the abovesaid Thomas Wresle & John Pilsworth to take care to dispose of the boy with Robert Berrier, & the agreement they make with him or any other this Meeting will see them indempnified & to give an account what they have done therein to the next Monthly Meeting.

p. 143.

Remember to search the Book what Jane Davis is behind for keeping Mary Codd & give account to the next Monthly Meeting.

The next Monthly Meeting to be at John Clark house in Garthorp.

[1] 12th July, 1689.

Att a Monthly Meeting held at John Clarkes in Garthorp the 9th day of the 6th month 1689[1] :—

One of Widdow Browne children that was with Robert Berrier of Ealand is put by this meeting to John Pilsworth of Belton the first day of the 6th month 89.[2] And it is left to the consideration of Friends at the next Monthly Meeting, what he shall have with him.

Ordered that a contribution be collected & brought into the next Monthly Meeting which is ordered to be at Brigge.

Signed by Joseph Richardson.

Att a Monthly Meeting held at Brigge the 13th of the 7th month 1689[3] :—

Contributions came in as followeth :

	£	s.	d.
Gainsbrough	00	12	10
Crowle	00	14	00
Winteringham	00	16	03
Brigge	00	13	06
Garthrop	00	09	00
	03	05	7
In Stock ..	00	05	6

Disburst to Thomas Wresle of Butterwick for Jane Davis of Belton for the keeping of Mary Codd the sum of one pound which makes up £02 : 15 : 00 for this last yeare ending the 16th day of this 7th month 1689[4] & alsoe paid the same time 5*s*. 6*d*. more which was laid downe for close & other repaires soe that there will rest yet unpaid 10*s* for the full of this year.

	£	s.	d.
To Thomas Wresle Botterwick for 2 poor Widdowes the sum of		05	7
To the Quarterly Meeting ordered	02	00	00

soe that nothing remaines in stock.

The next Monthly Meeting ordered to be at Thomas Wresles in Botterwick.

p. 144.

Att a Monthly Meeting held at the house of Thomas Wresles in Botterwick the 11th day of the 8th month 1689[5] :

Whereas it came under consideration in this Meeting, what every Perticular may raise towards defraying the charge of publick

[1] 9th August, 1689. [2] 1st August, 1689. [3] 13th September, 1689.
[4] 16th September, 1689. [5] 11th October, 1689.

Meeting house for the county in the city of Lincolne, Freinds of this Meeting thinks it meet that Gainsbrough, the Ile, Brigg & Winteringham Meetings raise each of them five marks apeice & that Garthrop Meeting raise thirty three shillings & four pence, which will be in all the sum of £15 : 00 : 00 to be collected & brought up to the next monthly Meetinge.

It is desired by this Meeting that Freinds draw up an account of what they have suffered for tythe this year & bring up to the next Meetinge.

This Meeting has agreed with John Pilsworth, senr. in Belton to table John Brown son to Happy Browne Widdow lately deceased, that he shall have three pounds a year for his table to enter the first day of the 6th month 1689[1] :—

Ordered the next Monthly Meeting be held at Brigge.

Signed by Joseph Richardson.

Att a Monthly Meeting held at Brigg the 8th of the 9th month 1689[2] :—

Contributions for the Meeting house at Lincolne came in as followeth :

	£	s.	d.
Gainsbrough	03	06	8
Winteringham	03	06	8
Brigg	03	06	8
Crowle	03	06	8
Garthrop	01	13	4
Totall ..	15	00	00

which is left to Gainsbrough Friends to send to Lincolne the first opportunity for the service aforesaid.

Friends not bringing in there suffering for tythe into this Meeting it is desired they faile not to bring them to the next.

John Haudenby of Cotle Hall came into this Meeting & signified his intentions of marriage wth Hannah Reeder of the same & shee being present gave her consent, but it being the first time they are desired to wait Friends answer till the next Monthly Meeting which is to be att Brigg.

[1] 1st August, 1689. [2] 8th November, 1689.

p. 145.

Att a Monthly Meeting held at the house of Edward Gilliat at Brigg the 13th of the 10th month 1689[1] :—

Contributions came in as followeth :

	£	s.	d.
From Gainsbrough	00 :	13 :	10
Winteringham Meeting	00 :	14 :	00
Botterwick Meeting..	00 :	13 :	00
Brigg Meeting ..	00 :	14 :	00
Garthrop Meeting ..	00 :	08 :	06
	03 :	03 :	04
Disburst to Michaell Beacock by John Clark	01 :	00 :	00
Paid more by John Howell ..	01 :	03 :	04
Ordered to the Quarterly Meeting..	01 :	00 :	00

soe nothing remaines

Ordered that Thomas Wresle & William Harrison lye down ten shillings to Jane Davis of Belton, which will be in full of what was due the 16th of the 7th month 1689[2] .

John Haudenby of Cotlehall came a second time into this Meeting with Hannah Reeder of the same, & signified the continuance of there purpose of marriage each with other, & Friends findeing nothing to hinder there said intentions have left the consumation thereof to themselves with the advice of Friends according to the good order of Truth.

The next Monthly Meeting ordered to be at Brigge.

Joseph Richardson.

[1] 13th December, 1689. [2] 16th September, 1689.

INDEX OF PERSONS AND PLACES

INDEX OF SUBJECTS